PURPOSE MADE

12 steps to discovering your God-given purpose

and living an abundant life

SARAH RITCHIE

To our **Heavenly Father**.
Thank you for this extraordinary life and purpose that
you have given me, including all of the teachable moments
through which I have been able to help others.

To my husband, **Simon**.
Out of 7.8 billion people, God intended you for me, and me for you.
He got it right.

Contents

Introduction

In 2012 I spear-headed a group of old high school friends, to organise a school reunion cleverly disguised as a 'combined 40th birthday'. Driven by curiosity, I wanted to find out what kind of lives my old classmates were living and the type of adults they had become.

Thanks to social media and some serious networking I was able to track down around 400 of our 600 high school peers. One interesting outcome of this search was that almost everybody I came across was pretty much as I remembered them from high school, with similar personalities, and who had taken a predictable career path.

Our reunion event caused me to think – do people really change all that much as they get older? Might those personality traits go back even further than high school – to childhood perhaps?

I dug deeper. I sent out a questionnaire to a wide range of friends and family and asked them the following questions (you might like to answer them too):

QUESTION 1:

Think back to your childhood and early teenage years – the time before you needed to think about your future, choosing school subjects, or what you would do when you left school. This was the time when you could just be the unencumbered you.

1a What was your personality like as a child (up to 10 years old)?

1b What did you love to do as a child (up to 10 years old)?

1c What was your personality like as a young teenager (up to 15 years old)?

1d What did you love to do as a young teenager (up to 15 years old)?

Now think about your adult life.

2a What is your personality like now?

2b Do you feel that your personality has changed much since you
were a child?

2c What do you love to do now?

2d Can you see any similarities between what you love to do now and
what you loved to do as a child?

2e What career (or life) path did you eventually choose?

2f Do you feel that your career (or life) path followed closely to what
you loved to do when you were a child? Yes/No. Please explain:

2g If you could have a 'do-over' of your chosen career (or life) path,
would you have chosen differently? Yes/No. Please explain:

The results were almost unanimous. Things we loved to do as children often stayed with us into our adult years. Interests we held as a child often extended through to our university studies and jobs. Our personalities matured and became more socially-adept, but we remained essentially the same as in our youth.

The next question that bubbled to the surface was this one – were our personality traits and interests already part of us from (or even BEFORE) the day we were born? Bingo! And so the journey of *Purpose Made* began.

Are you still trying to figure out what God wants you to do with your life or find a purpose or meaning to your existence? If so, you are not alone; for my first 40 years, I was in a very similar state of confusion.

You can do personality tests – which should solidify what you already know about yourself. You can do gifts tests – which can be illuminating and help to place your abilities and things which motivate you within a biblical and church context. But where do you go to from there? The good news is that God has planted within you substantial clues to your pathway and purpose. *Purpose Made* and the 12 Steps of the *Purpose Discovery Wheel* will help you to unlock what God has already placed in your heart.

Did you know that you are here on this great big, beautiful planet, for a reason other than to eat, sleep, work and consume oxygen? God knew all about you before you were born (He created you!) and our loving Heavenly Father doesn't make mistakes or forget things. You are who you are and where you are, on purpose.

Purpose Made will help you to figure out your way forward and discover God's plan for your life. You will then be better able to understand your fit and mandate within the church; your circle of influence (e.g. your workplace, your family and your friends); and your wider world beyond. Once you identify your purpose, you become perfectly poised to make your unique contribution, and that's an exciting thought!

BUT I'M NOT A CHRISTIAN...

You may be reading this book and do not subscribe to the Christian faith, or perhaps any faith. You may be wondering whether the content of this book is going to be appropriate for you.

Can you work your way through *Purpose Made* and the *Purpose Discovery Wheel* without having a Christian faith? The answer is most definitely "*yes*". Will it be confronting for you? Possibly. Will you get offended? That's up to you and how you choose to respond to what you read. If you approach the process with an open mind and open heart, then I am confident that you will see benefit and value by the time you reach the end of Step 12. The choice is now up to you!

Here's to LEANING INTO God, and LIVING IN your purpose!

SARAH RITCHIE

"No man need be a mediocrity if he accepts himself as God made him."

Patrick Kavanagh

When I read books by Christian authors, I tend to wonder whether their theology aligns with my own and whether I can 'trust' what they write. Therefore, I want to share, with you, my personal statement of faith, so that you might understand my beliefs and my heart right from the beginning of our journey together.

Rather than use my own words, I have borrowed the words from one of my favourite songs of all time – '*Creed*', by American Christian band, Petra. This song is particularly fitting, not just for the powerful declaration contained in the lyrics, but because my love of music and lyrics gives you a little insight into what makes me, me – as this book will help to illuminate what makes you, you. So, let's kick things off!

I believe in God the Father, maker of heaven and earth.
And in Jesus Christ His only Son, I believe in the virgin birth.
I believe in the Man of Sorrows, bruised for iniquities.
I believe in the Lamb who was crucified, and hung between two thieves.

I believe in the resurrection on the third and glorious day.
And I believe in the empty tomb and the stone that the angel rolled away.
He descended and set the captives free.
And now He sits at God's right hand, and prepares a place for me.

I believe He sent His Spirit to comfort and to reveal.
To lead us into the truth and light, to baptise and to seal.
I believe that He will come back the way He went away.
And receive us all unto Himself, but no man knows the day.

I believe He is the Judge of all men, small and great.
The resurrected souls of men receive from Him their fate.
Some to death and some to life, some to their reward.
Some to sing eternal praise forever to our Lord.

This is my creed, the witness I have heard.
The faith that has endured.
This truth is assured.
Through the darkest ages past, though persecuted, it will last.
And I will hold steadfast to this creed.

'*Creed*', recorded by Petra
Lyrics and music: Bob Hartman
©1990 Peermusic Publishing

Definitions

A book all about 'gifts' and 'purpose' needs to start with a few definitions. There are some words (including these two) which get used in various ways, so it is prudent for me to define how I intend to apply pivotal words throughout this book. If in doubt of my meaning, at any point in our journey together, please refer back to this section.

PURPOSE

We can use the word 'purpose' as either a noun (a naming word) or a verb (a doing word), and we will use both parts of speech throughout this book.

'Purpose', as used in the title of this book, is the noun form of the word, which means:

- The reason something is done or created, or for which something exists.

Other definitions of the word 'purpose' (also nouns) which are relevant and will be used throughout this book are:

- An intended or desired result; end; aim; or goal (e.g. "*I finished early for the express purpose of attending the event*").
- Determination; resoluteness (e.g. come to a decision or settle a 'purpose').

The verb definitions are also highly relevant and will be used within this book (including 'purposed' and 'purposing'), and include:

- To set as an aim, intention, or goal for oneself (e.g. "*I will purpose to do this*").
- To intend; design (e.g. "*God purposed you*").
- To have a purpose (e.g. to propose as an aim or plan to oneself).

GIFT

A 'gift' (noun) as everyone from childhood and up knows, is a 'present' – a thing that is given willingly to someone without payment. It can also refer to natural ability or talent (e.g. *"She has a gift for singing"*). *Purpose Made* is all about the present-type of gifts, and specifically, those given to us directly by God, Jesus Christ and the Holy Spirit. We will refer to the talent type of gifts as 'talents', to avoid any confusion.

TALENT

The word 'talent' is a pretty simple one to describe and grasp, and we talk about talents all the time in our modern language – *"She has so many talents"*; *"You could see he was talented from a young age"* and so forth.

The dictionary definition of 'talent' (noun) is a natural aptitude or skill, and 'talented' (adjective or describing word) refers to having a natural aptitude or skill.

We should not confuse the meaning, above, with the word 'talent' as it is often used in the Bible where it describes a weight and unit of currency of the ancient Greeks and Romans.

PASSION

The word 'passion' needs to be defined more carefully, as it has several different meanings and interpretations, especially within our modern culture.

Within this book, I will be using 'passion' to describe an intense desire or enthusiasm for something (as opposed to someone); or a thing that inspires great enthusiasm.

We also have to be careful that we do not confuse our definition with the use of 'Passion' as it refers to the suffering and death of Jesus. 'Passion' (the pronoun) comes from the Latin word for suffering – the complete opposite of what we will be diving into together!

ANOINTING

The word 'anointing' describes the application of oil as a sign of consecration or sanctification, which we see in practise throughout the Bible (for the appointment of prophets, priests and kings). 'Anointing' also refers to the official choice of a person to do an important job, or designating someone as the 'chosen one'.

The pinnacle example of this is Jesus Christ and illustrated when Jesus read from the book of Isaiah in the synagogue in Nazareth, Israel. He read: "*The Spirit of the Lord is upon Me because He anointed Me to preach the gospel to the poor. He has sent Me to proclaim release to the captives, and recovery of sight to the blind, to set free those who are oppressed, to proclaim the favourable year of the Lord.*" (Luke 4:18–19, NASB)

1 John 2:20 (NASB) says, "*But you have an anointing from the Holy One, and you know all things.*" The 'you' whom the apostle John was addressing were the Believers and followers of Jesus Christ (Christians), and he referred to them – generally – as having an anointing.

Why are we here?

Have you ever wondered why people are born, only to die some 70 or 80 years later? If you have an atheistic world view (where you don't believe in the existence of God), you probably don't care about the question very much and prefer to live by an 'anything goes, because you only live once' philosophy.

If you have a Christian world view, then you probably care a great deal and have also contemplated why God created human beings in the first place and why we are living in such a broken world.

As you will find out – by the end of this book – each one of us has a unique reason for being on this planet, which I am calling your 'purpose'; and God has designed every one of our individual purposes to dovetail with His greater purpose for humankind. It is, therefore, essential for us to understand what God's intentions are, so we can make sure that our thoughts, words and actions are all in alignment with His bigger picture.

TO FELLOWSHIP WITH GOD

We read in the very first chapter of the Bible (Genesis 1) that in the beginning, God created the heavens, the earth, vegetation, animals, and man and woman. The Bible tells us that God specifically created man in His image and that He desired to have 'fellowship' (companionship, friendship) with His creation.

Genesis 1:28 (NIV) also says that *"God blessed them and said to them, "Be fruitful and increase in number; fill the earth and subdue it. Rule over the fish in the sea and the birds in the sky and over every living creature that moves on the ground."* God not only designed for mankind to be in fellowship with Him, He desired that man would look after the animals and the garden that He had created (Genesis 2:15).

When the first people – Adam and Eve – rebelled and disobeyed God's word of instruction, sin entered and spoiled the new world that God had created. Adam and Eve's sin brought with it the consequence of death, and death spread to everyone. Every human being (having descended from Adam) inherited Adam's sin-nature, which meant that our original sinless fellowship with God was cut off, because God is holy and we became sinful. Thus, a great separation took place.

Mercifully, God had made a way for us to return to fellowship with Him (and atone for our sins), through the death and resurrection of His Son, Jesus Christ.

"God made him who had no sin to be sin for us so that in him we might become the righteousness of God." (2 Corinthians 5:21, NIV). This verse explains how God acted in love for our sake, to make it possible to remove the separation between Him and us, which was our sin. To accomplish this, God gave us Jesus Christ, who had never sinned during His life on earth in any way. Jesus' death on the cross paid the price for our sin, removing our guilt and removing the obstacle of sin between God and us. Those who come to God through faith in Jesus Christ are given credit for Jesus' righteous, sinless life. We *"become God's righteousness"* and are reconciled in our relationship with Him.

*"The God who made the world and everything in it is the Lord of heaven and earth and does not live in temples built by human hands. And He is not served by human hands, as if he needed anything. Rather, He himself gives everyone life and breath and everything else. From one man He made all the nations, that they should inhabit the whole earth; and **He marked out their appointed times in history** and the boundaries of their lands. God did this so that they would seek Him and perhaps reach out for Him*

and find Him, though He is not far from any one of us." (Acts 17:24–27, NIV, emphasis added)

Why are we here on earth? We are here to praise God; to seek and find Him and to be found by Him; to be reconciled with God through Jesus Christ; to better understand and appreciate who He is, and to help others find that same relationship with Him that we have found, so that – ultimately – we can all spend eternity with Him.

TO BE LIKE JESUS

We know that God created mankind in His image, including His character. However, through the sinful act of Adam and Eve, it then became impossible for mankind to reflect the perfect nature of God.

By God sending His only Son, Jesus, He was not only providing a way for the atonement of our sins, but He was also giving us a role model that we could emulate. Jesus lived for around 33 years on this earth, and the Bible records much detail about the last few years of His life and ministry. In John 14:7 (NIV) Jesus himself said: "*If you really know me, you will know my Father as well.*" Through reading the Bible (God's Word to us), we can better understand Jesus' life, teachings and actions; discover more about the character of God, and how to live the best life possible.

John 17 contains an epic prayer that Jesus prayed to His heavenly Father just before he set out for the Garden of Gethsemane, which then led to His arrest, crucifixion and resurrection. This chapter gives us great insight into the heart, glory, plan and will of God.

If we know that one of the reasons we are on this earth is to learn to be more like Jesus, then we should take advice from the prayer He prayed. In John 17:4 (NIV) Jesus said, "*I have brought you [God] glory on earth by finishing the work you gave me to do.*"

Let that also be our prayer. That we can live our lives for God and bring glory to His name through our thoughts, words, worship and actions – always shining the light on Him; and that we may finish the work (our purpose, plans and assignments) which God has prepared for us to do.

Why are we here on earth? To learn to model our lives and conduct on Jesus; to show Jesus in the flesh to others, and to bring Jesus' love, reconciliation and healing ministry to a world in pain. We do this to be a reflection of God's nature and ultimately bring glory to God.

TO HELP ESTABLISH GOD'S KINGDOM

Even if you are not a Christian, you have probably heard about The Lord's Prayer, which you'll find in the book of Matthew. Jesus was teaching His disciples how to pray, and He said "*and when you pray, do not keep on babbling like pagans, for they think they will be heard because of their many words. Do not be like them, for your Father knows what you need before you ask Him. This, then, is how you should pray:*
Our Father in heaven, hallowed be your name,
your kingdom come, your will be done, *on earth as it is in heaven.*
Give us today our daily bread.
And forgive us our debts, as we also have forgiven our debtors.
And lead us not into temptation, but deliver us from the evil one."
(Matthew 6:7–13, NIV, emphasis added)

That's a pretty short prayer, so you can bet your money that Jesus was covering off all the essentials. We've all uttered this line many times, "your kingdom come, your will be done, on earth as it is in heaven" but what are we praying for, and what has it got to do with God's greater purpose for us?

The message of the entire Bible (from beginning to end, Genesis to Revelation) is that God wants to restore the world to His original design (pre-Adam's sin), with no more war, sickness, injustice or brokenness.

What God wants, desires and wills is His good and perfect kingdom. His kingdom is not come in its fullness or completeness, yet, on the earth, but it's His wish, and He wants it to be our joy and desire too.

Jesus' message was that the kingdom of God was at hand. The gospel of the kingdom (which Jesus preached, also called the 'Good News'), is that – through death – Jesus went from the messenger bringing the good news of God's kingdom, to the king who would reign over it. He conquered over sin and death and the Evil One, and He established a way by which all of His followers could take part in the kingdom of God.

Before He went to the cross, Jesus prayed in Luke 22:42 (NIV): "*Father, if you are willing, take this cup from me; yet not my will, but yours be done.*" If there was any other way than to die for the sins of the world, Jesus could have taken it. But He voluntarily laid down His life for you and me.

At His first coming, Jesus presented Himself as a Suffering Servant to die for the sins of the world. At His Second Coming, Jesus is returning as the King and Judge. He is not coming as a baby in a manger but as the Judge to judge the world. God's kingdom will not be entirely on the earth until Jesus returns.

To pray "*your kingdom come, your will be done*" is to look forward to the day when God's will is completed on the earth and when God Himself will dwell with mankind as was His original design in the beginning.

Why are we here on earth?
- To help and support the establishment of God's kingdom – by praying as Jesus instructed, and by demonstrating what kingdom life can look like, using Jesus as our example.
- To pray that God's will be done (on earth as it is in heaven), which includes God's will for your own life. You will never be able to comprehend God's bigger picture, so all you can do is be faithful to see God's will done in your own life, trusting that He will fit all the pieces of the jigsaw puzzle together in His own time and His own way.

Why it's important to know your purpose

We live in a world where it can be challenging to find a sense of hope or peace. It can also be difficult to understand where you fit into the confusion that swirls around you.

In the previous section we looked at the reasons why God made people in the first place; the reasons why we all still exist on the earth today; and how God intends individual plans to fit snuggly into His overall plan for His people.

It's essential for each Bible-believing, God-fearing Christian to have a clear understanding about why they exist on this planet, and how God wants to use their lives to bless others and honour Him. So, why is it so essential to understand your God-given purpose?

TO LIVE AN ABUNDANT LIFE

Jesus said, "*The thief comes only to steal and kill and destroy; I have come that they may have life, and have it to the full.*" (John 10:10, NIV). Without a clear sense of meaning or purpose it's easy to drift through your days, running on the same hamster wheel of life: wake-up —> eat —> travel —> work or study —> travel —> eat —> watch TV —> sleep; rinse and repeat. If that's all there is, then that is the antithesis of living an abundant life, so it's time to put the brakes on that hamster wheel and make a radical change.

To live in abundance, your life needs a captain (Jesus), a destination (your purpose) and a course (your assignments – how your purpose will be outworked). As you make your way through the *Purpose Discovery Wheel*, later in this book, you should tangibly feel your life moving from 'average' to 'abundant'.

TO LIVE A RENEWED LIFE

Have you ever wondered why our suicide statistics are so high? If people (especially our youth) do not know their purpose, then they may see death as a more attractive option to living. Loneliness is not a lack of company; it's a lack of purpose. Depression does not require medication; it requires purpose. Feeling a lack of direction or hopelessness in your life is also a lack of purpose.

Suicide, loneliness, depression and hopelessness have no place in God's will for His children. If you believe that Jesus Christ died for your sins, and if you renounce your past and press into God to guide your future, then you too are His child, and can live a renewed life through Him – and that's a promise!

TO LIVE A LIFE WITH DIRECTION

Proverbs 29:18 (KJV) says "*where there is no vision, the people perish.*"

One interpretation of this verse is 'where there is no perspective from God's point of view the people will run wild'. Without a clear and meaningful godly vision to follow it's way too easy to veer off-course (or 'run wild'). Going off-track means wasted time, consequences or worse.

Another way to look at this verse is being smart about where you invest your time. American businesswoman Caterina Fake said "*Much more important than working hard is knowing how to find the right thing to work on.*" Without a clear vision (or purpose), we can invest countless hours working extremely hard, but concentrating on the wrong things.

TO LIVE A FRUITFUL LIFE

"When you love something, you work harder at it. When you work harder at it, success comes. "(Bobby Bones, American Idol 2018).

Have you ever done something, but your heart wasn't really in it, and so your results were marginal? When you are 'in the zone' (walking in your God-given purpose), you will automatically be doing something you love (because that's how purpose works), and you will be propelled along by what I call your 'fire'. Your 'fire' drives you to work hard, doing what you love, in an area that God's called you to, on a specific assignment. Then, boom! All of a sudden, the fruit will follow.

By knowing what your purpose is, then being faithful to see it through, you will find your life burst forth with all kinds of fruit. This fruit can include energy, fulfilment, commitment, positivity, direction, enjoyment, joy, a sense of belonging, love for others, productivity, and results. Worth it? I think so!

One purpose or many?

Let's look at the biblical account of King David, which can be found primarily in the books 1 & 2 Samuel. David is one of the most referenced people in the Bible with sixty-six chapters dedicated to his story. According to scripture, the key moments of David's life can be summed up as follows:

- He was a shepherd in his youth.
- He defeated the giant champion, Goliath.
- He was a poet and harp player, and is attributed to writing 75 of the 150 psalms in the Bible.
- He worked as an aide at the court of Saul, Israel's first king.
- He became a favourite of King Saul and was a friend of Saul's son, Jonathan.
- He distinguished himself as a warrior against the Philistines.
- Saul turned on David when he thought David intended to take his throne.
- David fled to southern Judah and Philistia where he began to lay the foundations of his career.
- He became the leader and organiser of a group of outlaws and refugees, and gradually assimilated with the local population living a 'Robin Hood-esque' existence.
- After Saul and Jonathan died in combat, David was chosen to be the second king of Israel.

- He had to wait to assume his kingship while Saul's son – Ishbaal – laid claim to the throne of his father.
- Ishbaal was murdered by his courtiers, then David was anointed king.
- He then captured Jerusalem, brought the Ark of the Covenant into the city, and secured the kingdom founded by Saul.
- He defeated the Philistines so thoroughly that they were never again a serious threat to Israel.
- He committed adultery with Bathsheba and arranged the death of her husband, Uriah the Hittite.
- Because of his sin, God refused David the possibility of building the temple.
- David's son Absalom tried to overthrow him.
- He escaped Jerusalem during Absalom's revolt and returned to rule Israel after Absalom's death.
- Before he died, David anointed his son Solomon as his heir.

If you look at David's key moments, would you say that God had one purpose for David's life or multiple purposes over the years? The answer essentially comes down to semantics and the words people use to describe concepts, especially where we can interchange two or more different words to mean the same thing.

In the journey to write *Purpose Made*, I have deliberately chosen specific words to have specific meanings. As you have already read, my use of the word 'purpose' is to describe the reason something (in this case, you) exists.

Your 'purpose' is not one specific 'thing', but a culmination of many things brought together that make up the intricate picture of who you are, and the plans that God has for your life.

As you make your way through the *Purpose Discovery Wheel* (later on in this book) you will see that your purpose is a mix of your personality, gifts, talents, loves, bankable skills; the world around you; your 'fire', job, calling and assignments. Phew, that's a lot of elements in there!

Purpose can also change and evolve. While some purpose-related factors in your life may never change, things like your 'fire', job, calling, and assignments will most certainly change over time. Does that then mean that you have multiple purposes? No, it just means your overall, God-given purpose will naturally evolve.

If we look at the example of David, one could summarise that David's life-purpose was to be an inspiring, God-fearing, law-abiding leader. We can then see how God was training David, through a series of jobs and assignments, to build him up to one day be King of Israel.

For example, as a 14-year-old boy, David was a shepherd who looked after his family's flock of sheep. In 1 Samuel 17:31–36, David tells Saul that he had killed both a lion and a bear to protect those sheep. These youthful experiences gave David the confidence that he could step out and face Goliath in battle, which he did. David killed Goliath with just his shepherd's slingshot and a smooth stone.

David's victory over Goliath was the entry point for him working in Saul's court, where we also know that David was able to use his boyhood talent for harp-playing to soothe Saul's troubled mind.

If you look at David's life, his various experiences and assignments dovetailed into one another. Over the years, David was able to build up his spiritual muscle, resilience and life experience to the point where God could confidently appoint him as king. David is an excellent example of having (for the most part) followed a godly path with one overarching purpose; multiple assignments; highs, lows and detours; and a lifetime of development and training.

Let's illustrate the idea of purpose in a modern context using an athlete we will call Joe. Joe is a top-level shot put champion who has competed in the last two Olympic Games.

Joe was probably really good at sports when he was a child and teenager. He may have dreamed of one day walking across the field in a crowded Olympic stadium, but when 12-year-old Joe declared to his parents *"I'm going to be an Olympic athlete"* you can bet that the next day he wasn't hopping on board a plane bound for the Olympic Village.

Joe built up his abilities over many years. He competed first for his school, then his college and then his country. He experienced ups and downs, battling through injuries and seasons of discouragement, until one day he qualified for the Olympic Games.

One might look at Joe's life and think that his purpose is to be an Olympic athlete, but God sees things differently to the way that man sees them. In God's eyes, Joe's purpose is to impact and influence the international sports community for God. To this end, you could think of the Olympic Games as like a 'job', where Joe worked his way up the ladder to reach the pinnacle of his sports career. Therefore, the Olympic Games was not the end destination, it was a stepping stone, and Joe will move on from there to other jobs or assignments or callings to reach people in and around the sports world for God.

Science proves it; you are 100% unique!

When we read through the Scriptures, we can build up a clear picture of how much God loves us and how intricately and intentionally we have been created. Throughout *Purpose Made*, we will look at many of the Bible verses which illustrate the extent to which God regards you as a masterpiece.

While some people are happy to rely on the Word of God to tell them how special they are, others require more physical 'proof'.

We are blessed to live in a time where science has made all sorts of new and exciting discoveries that prove you are a one-of-a-kind, unique human being.

So, please pop on your lab coat and join me on a scientific detour into the wonderful and complex world of anatomy and physiology.

DNA

DNA is also known as 'deoxyribonucleic acid', the molecules in cells that determine the genetic characteristics of all life. It takes the form of a double helix (two strands coiled together).

DNA was first discovered in the 19th century, and by the 1940s, scientists realised that DNA contained 'the code for life'.

DNA is what makes your body tick and – because we are not clones – the genome of every human is unique.

It all starts with your genes. The four-letter code that provides the blueprint of your body is unlike anyone else's and is made up of nucleotides A-G-C-T (adenine, guanine, cytosine and thymine).

Each cell in your body contains around 3,200,000,000 (yes, that's 3.2 billion) nucleotide pairs, and your body contains around 20,000–25,000 genes. When you look at genetics this way, it's perhaps not surprising to think that your genetic code may influence more than just your hair texture and eye colour.

There is a lot more information in your genes than just appearance and hereditary diseases. Genes encode proteins that have many functions throughout the body. They help determine your body's metabolic processes, which is the sum of the chemical reactions that keep you alive.

Genes encode the number and shape of receptors on your cells that respond to chemical signals like insulin, opioids, and cortisol. Not to mention your sensory receptors, which explains why some people can't stand coriander and others may sneeze when exposed to bright light.

A 'genetic fingerprint' is the pattern of DNA unique to each individual, which can be analysed and used as a means of identification (familiar to all you crime novel fans out there).

Genetic fingerprints exist in blood, bone, hair follicles, saliva, semen, skin and sweat. They are the same in every cell and retain their distinctiveness throughout a person's life.

Apart from identification, paternity and immigration cases, the genetic fingerprinting technique is also used in medical research.

The sphere of influence of your DNA is vast, and your DNA is 100% all yours!

MICROBIOME

Trillions of bacterial cells live inside your large intestine, and their activities influence your whole-body health, not just your gut.

There's about 1.5 kg of bacteria living in your colon right now, but until recently, scientists couldn't see what they were doing. It's DNA sequencing technology that has made it possible to screen your stool and identify the bacterial genes in it.

Every person's gut microbiome is a unique ecosystem with a multitude of different bacteria doing an array of tasks you wouldn't have thought possible. Research now indicates that they start to colonise your gut before you even leave the womb!

In newborns and infants, their first job is to train your immune system, which learns to differentiate between helpful bacteria and pathogens. Once the microbiome is fully developed and you're grown it takes care of a lot of functions, such as modulating your immune system; maintaining the lining of your intestinal tract; and ensuring the correct pH in your large intestine.

Now that you know what a microbiome is, you can also live happily in the knowledge that your microbiome is yours alone!

FINGERPRINTS

For centuries, scholars had remarked on the curious loops and 'whorls' of ridged skin on the tips of their fingers. The 'prints' themselves are the patterns of skin oils or dirt these ridges leave behind on a surface that you've touched.

In 1788, the scientist J.C.A. Mayers declared that the patterns seemed unique and that *"the arrangement of skin ridges is never duplicated in two persons."* It was an interesting observation, but one that lay dormant until 19th-century society began to grapple with an emerging problem: how do you prove people are who they say they are? Methods to identify people using their fingerprints developed over the following decades.

Fingerprints begin to form before you are born. When a baby starts to grow, the outside layer of its skin is smooth. But after about ten weeks, a deeper layer of skin, called the basal layer, starts growing faster than the layers above it, which makes it 'buckle' and fold. The expanding lower layer ends up scrunched and bunched beneath the outside layer. These folds eventually cause the surface layers of the skin to fold too, and by the time a baby is 17 weeks old (about halfway through pregnancy) its fingerprints are set.

Although this folding process might sound random, the genes you get from your parents influence the overall size and shape of your fingerprints; so you probably share some fingerprint similarities with your family members.

But the details of your fingerprints are all yours! No two people end up with the same fingerprints, even identical twins.

It was only in 2015 that a long-term study showed that fingerprints are stable over a person's lifetime. The ridges of a fingerprint are visible on the skin's surface layer, but the pattern is actually 'encoded' below that. Even if you have major skin injury, your prints will come back when the outer layer heals.

Science proves it – your fingerprints are completely unique to you and have been since before you were born.

Isn't God incredible!

"In Him we were also chosen, having been predestined according to the plan of Him who works out everything in conformity with the purpose of His will…"
(Ephesians 1:11, NIV)

WHAT DOES 'PREDESTINATION' MEAN?

'Predestination' means that God is able to 'predetermine' the 'destiny' of people and events, long in advance of them coming to pass. In your case, that means that God has already mapped out His good and perfect plan for your life, which can be a pretty mind-blowing thought, and often difficult to accept or understand.

Predestination does not mean the absence of choice. God never created you to be His puppet. He has given you a free will and the ability to make your own decisions.

At times you will choose wisely and remain on the path that God has pre-planned for you. Other times you will make choices that put a kink in your path or cause you to veer off in a different direction.

The good news is that the Bible says (in Romans 8:28) that "*God causes ALL things to work together…*" He can take our misjudgement, mistakes, ill-considered choices and even deliberately sinful decisions that we make and weave them back into the beautiful design that He has for our lives – even if it takes a while for us to get back on track.

Assuming that you accept the notion that your life is predestined, the big question then becomes WHEN did God make this plan for you? Is He making it up as you go along, tweaking it every time you make a good or bad decision? To solve this rather large question, we have to turn to the Bible for the answer.

Throughout Scripture, we read about God knowing and planning things, and then sharing that information directly to the person concerned, or conveying the message via someone else (such as a prophet).

Both the Old and New Testaments of the Bible contain accounts of individuals who were predestined to fulfil a divine purpose. Jeremiah (Jeremiah 1:5) writes of God knowing him before he was formed in the womb and being set apart before he was born to be a prophet to the nations. Isaiah (Isaiah 49:5) writes that he is conscious of being *"formed in the womb to be His* [God's] *servant."* In Genesis 25:23 God tells Isaac's wife, Rebekah, the destiny of her unborn twin sons – Jacob and Esau. In the New Testament, the Apostle Paul speaks of himself as set apart from birth to know God's Son and to make Him known (Galatians 1:15-16).

Paul also writes about predestination in the book of Romans: *"And we know that God causes all things to work together for good to those who love God, to those who are called according to His purpose. For those whom He foreknew, He also predestined to become conformed to the image of His Son, so that He would be the firstborn among many brethren; and these whom He predestined, He also called; and these whom He called, He also justified; and these whom He justified, He also glorified."* (Romans 8:28–30, NASB).

Predestination is all about two important things. Firstly, God has devised a specific plan and purpose for you. And, secondly, He made that plan not ad hoc throughout your life; not on the day of your birth; not even as you were developing in your mother's womb, but BEFORE YOU WERE EVEN CONCEIVED.

You have been cherished by God for a very, very long time. Your birth happened at just the right time in history because God intended it to be that way. This fact alone means that you can NEVER regard your birth as an accident (no matter who your parents are, or the circumstances around your conception). Let that sink into your soul for a moment.

WHERE IS THE PROOF?

To find the proof for predestination before conception, we again need to look to the Bible. The Scriptures give us examples of people whose birth was foretold hundreds of years before the actual event.

The most notable of these prophetic words pertain to the birth, life and ministry of Jesus Christ. The Bible records a staggering 100+ prophecies made between 400 years and 1,500 years before His birth, all of which came to pass exactly as written.

You might say *"but, yes, Jesus was the Son of God, and He was special."* You are quite right, so let's dig further to see if we can find some examples of 'mere mortals' whose lives were foretold or predestined in the same way.

The following passages of Scripture show five stand-out examples of predestination before conception.

ISAAC

Isaac was the son of Abraham, the father of Jacob, and a direct ancestor of Jesus Christ. He lived around 1896 BC to 1716 B.C., and here is the account of Isaac's birth foretold (Genesis 18:1–14, NIV).

"The Lord appeared to Abraham near the great trees of Mamre while he was sitting at the entrance to his tent in the heat of the day. Abraham looked up and saw three men standing nearby. When he saw them, he hurried from the entrance of his tent to meet them and bowed low to the ground.

"He said, "If I have found favour in your eyes, my Lord, do not pass your servant by. Let a little water be brought, and then you may all wash your feet and rest under this tree. Let me get you something to eat, so you can be refreshed and then go on your way—now that you have come to your servant." "Very well," they answered, "do as you say."

"So Abraham hurried into the tent to Sarah. "Quick," he said, "get three

seahs of the finest flour and knead it and bake some bread.”

Then he ran to the herd and selected a choice, tender calf and gave it to a servant, who hurried to prepare it. He then brought some curds and milk and the calf that had been prepared and set these before them. While they ate, he stood near them under a tree.

““Where is your wife Sarah?” they asked him. “There, in the tent,” he said. Then one of them said, “I will surely return to you about this time next year, and Sarah your wife will have a son.”

“Now Sarah was listening at the entrance to the tent, which was behind him. Abraham and Sarah were already very old, and Sarah was past the age of childbearing. So Sarah laughed to herself as she thought, “After I am worn out and my lord is old, will I now have this pleasure?”

“Then the Lord said to Abraham, “Why did Sarah laugh and say, ‘Will I really have a child, now that I am old?’ Is anything too hard for the Lord? I will return to you at the appointed time next year, and Sarah will have a son.”””

SAMSON

You are probably familiar with the biblical story of Samson and Delilah, which can be found in the book of Judges. Samson held the position of Judge in the land of Israel and lived around the time of 1120 B.C. Here is the biblical account of how the birth of Samson was foretold to his parents, before his conception (Judges 13, 2–5, NIV).

“A certain man of Zorah, named Manoah, from the clan of the Danites, had a wife who was childless, unable to give birth. The angel of the Lord appeared to her and said, “You are barren and childless, but you are going to become pregnant and give birth to a son. Now see to it that you drink no wine or other fermented drink and that you do not eat anything unclean. You will become pregnant and have a son whose head is never to be touched by a razor because the boy is to be a Nazirite, dedicated to God from the womb. He will take the lead in delivering Israel from the hands of the Philistines.”

KING JOSIAH

Josiah was a descendant of King David, the 15th king of the land of Judah and lived around 640 B.C.

The following prophecy was made during the reign of King Jeroboam (the 1st king of Israel) after the kingdom split in two following the reign of King Solomon. King Jeroboam reigned around 920 B.C. …300 years before Josiah was born!

(1 Kings 13:1–2, NIV)

"By the word of the Lord, a man of God came from Judah to Bethel, as Jeroboam was standing by the altar to make an offering. By the word of the Lord, he cried out against the altar: "Altar, altar! This is what the Lord says: 'A son named Josiah will be born to the house of David. On you, he will sacrifice the priests of the high places who make offerings here, and human bones will be burned on you.""

We read in 2 Chronicles 34:1–5 (NIV) the fulfilment of the prophecy:

"Josiah was eight years old when he became king, and he reigned in Jerusalem thirty-one years. He did what was right in the eyes of the Lord and followed the ways of his father David, not turning aside to the right or to the left."

KING CYRUS

In around 700 B.C., Isaiah wrote about a conqueror from the east, and in one of the most remarkable prophecies in all of Scripture, names the future Persian emperor (Cyrus). He described what Cyrus would do, 150 years before the event.

"Thus says the Lord, your Redeemer, who formed you from the womb:… who says of Cyrus, 'He is my shepherd, and he shall fulfil all my purpose'; saying of Jerusalem, 'She shall be built,' and of the temple, 'Your foundation shall be laid.'"

"Thus says the Lord to his anointed, to Cyrus, whose right hand I have grasped, to subdue nations before him and to loose the belts of kings, to open doors before him that gates may not be closed: "I will go before you and level the exalted places, I will break in pieces the doors of bronze and cut through

the bars of iron, I will give you the treasures of darkness and the hoards in secret places, that you may know that it is I, the Lord, the God of Israel, who calls you by your name.

"For the sake of my servant Jacob, and Israel my chosen, I call you by your name, I name you, though you do not know me. I am the Lord, and there is no other, besides me, there is no God; I equip you, though you do not know me, that people may know, from the rising of the sun and from the west, that there is none besides me; I am the Lord, and there is no other.

"I form light and create darkness; I make well-being and create calamity; I am the Lord, who does all these things.

"Shower, O heavens, from above, and let the clouds rain down righteousness; let the earth open, that salvation and righteousness may bear fruit; let the earth cause them both to sprout; I the Lord have created it.

"Woe to him who strives with him who formed him, a pot among earthen pots! Does the clay say to him who forms it, 'What are you making?' or 'Your work has no handles'? Woe to him who says to a father, 'What are you begetting?' or to a woman, 'With what are you in labour?'"

Thus says the Lord, the Holy One of Israel, and the one who formed him: "Ask me of things to come; will you command me concerning my children and the work of my hands? I made the earth and created man on it; it was my hands that stretched out the heavens, and I commanded all their host.

"I have stirred him up in righteousness, and I will make all his ways level; he shall build my city and set my exiles free, not for price or reward," says the Lord of hosts."

(Isaiah 44:24, 28; 45:1–6, ESV)

Cyrus is mentioned some twenty-three times in the Bible. Isaiah refers to Cyrus as Jehovah's "*shepherd*," the Lord's "*anointed*," who was providentially appointed to facilitate the divine plan. God would lead this monarch to "*subdue nations*" and "*open doors*" (an allusion to the release of the Jews from Babylonian captivity). He would make "*rough places smooth*" (accommodate the return of the Jewish people to their homeland in Israel). He would ultimately be responsible for the rebuilding of Jerusalem and the reconstruction of the temple.

Amazingly, King Cyrus would accomplish these noble tasks even though he did not *"know"* Jehovah God (Isaiah 45:4, 5). In other words, though he was a pagan in sentiment and practice, yet, as an unconscious tool in the hands of the Lord, he would be a major contributor to the Jewish cause, and so, indirectly, to the coming of God's greater Anointed, Jesus Christ.

We can read about the fulfilment of these specific predictions in 2 Chronicles 36:22, 23 and Ezra 1:1-4, 7, 8; 3:7; 4:3.

JOHN THE BAPTIST

John the Baptist (or John the Baptiser) is one of the most significant figures in the biblical Gospels. As was the case with Jesus Christ, his birth was prophesied in the Old Testament; meticulously recorded in Luke 1:5-25; not to mention marked by angelic proclamation and divine intervention (Luke 1:57-80).

There are three places, in the Old Testament, where John's purpose is foretold:

1 Isaiah 40:3-5 (NIV), written around 700 B.C.

"A voice of one calling in the wilderness prepare the way for the Lord; make straight in the desert a highway for our God. Every valley shall be raised up, every mountain and hill made low; the rough ground shall become level, the rugged places a plain. And the glory of the Lord will be revealed, and all people will see it together. For the mouth of the Lord has spoken."

How can we be 100% sure that this passage was about John the Baptist? Matthew 3:1–3 (NIV) confirms it: *"In those days John the Baptist came, preaching in the wilderness of Judea and saying, "Repent, for the kingdom of heaven has come near." This is he who was spoken of through the prophet Isaiah: "A voice of one calling in the wilderness, 'Prepare the way for the Lord, make straight paths for him.'"*

John himself acknowledged his connection with the prophecy. In John 1:19–23 (NIV):

"Now this was John's testimony when the Jewish leaders in Jerusalem

sent priests and Levites to ask him who he was. He did not fail to confess, but confessed freely, "I am not the Messiah." "They asked him, "Then who are you? Are you Elijah?" He said, "I am not." "Are you the Prophet?" He answered, "No." Finally, they said, "Who are you? Give us an answer to take back to those who sent us. What do you say about yourself?" John replied in the words of Isaiah the prophet, "I am the voice of one calling in the wilderness, 'Make straight the way for the Lord.'"

2   Malachi 3:1 (NIV), written around 430 B.C.

The prophet Malachi, like Isaiah, spoke of John's role in preparing the way of Jesus Christ, the Messiah.

"I will send my messenger, who will prepare the way before me. Then suddenly the Lord you are seeking will come to his temple; the messenger of the covenant, whom you desire, will come," says the Lord Almighty."

Again, how can we be sure that this is a reference to John? Because Jesus said so in Matthew 11:7–10 (NIV):

"As John's disciples were leaving, Jesus began to speak to the crowd about John: "What did you go out into the wilderness to see? A reed swayed by the wind? If not, what did you go out to see? A man dressed in fine clothes? No, those who wear fine clothes are in kings' palaces. Then what did you go out to see? A prophet? Yes, I tell you, and more than a prophet. This is the one about whom it is written: "'I will send my messenger ahead of you, who will prepare your way before you.'"

3   Malachi 4:5 (NIV), written around 430 B.C.

"See, I will send the prophet Elijah to you before that great and dreadful day of the Lord comes."

How can it be true that John was Elijah, the great prophet of Israel who lived over 800 years before John? As with the two other Old Testament passages, the New Testament gives us a clear explanation. Jesus Christ said in Matthew 11:13–14 (NIV), *"For all the Prophets and the Law prophesied until John. And if you are willing to accept it, he is the Elijah who was to come."*

Not only was John's ministry recorded hundreds of years before it happened, but his parents also received a prophetic word about his imminent conception and birth. This account is recorded in Luke 1:5–17 (NIV).

"In the time of Herod king of Judea there was a priest named Zechariah, who belonged to the priestly division of Abijah; his wife Elizabeth was also a descendant of Aaron. Both of them were righteous in the sight of God, observing all the Lord's commands and decrees blamelessly. But they were childless because Elizabeth was not able to conceive, and they were both very old.

"Once when Zechariah's division was on duty, and he was serving as priest before God, he was chosen by lot, according to the custom of the priesthood, to go into the temple of the Lord and burn incense. And when the time for the burning of incense came, all the assembled worshipers were praying outside.

"Then an angel of the Lord appeared to him, standing at the right side of the altar of incense. When Zechariah saw him, he was startled and was gripped with fear. But the angel said to him: "Do not be afraid, Zechariah; your prayer has been heard. Your wife Elizabeth will bear you a son, and you are to call him John. He will be a joy and delight to you, and many will rejoice because of his birth, for he will be great in the sight of the Lord. He is never to take wine or other fermented drink, and he will be filled with the Holy Spirit even before he is born. He will bring back many of the people of Israel to the Lord their God. And he will go on before the Lord, in the spirit and power of Elijah, to turn the hearts of the parents to their children and the disobedient to the wisdom of the righteous — to make ready a people prepared for the Lord."

Jesus Christ himself said of John: *"Truly I tell you, among those born of women there has not risen anyone greater than John the Baptist; yet whoever is least in the kingdom of heaven is greater than he."* (Matthew 11:11, NIV). John is clearly a pivotal figure in the salvation narrative of God, **whose destiny was foretold 700 years before he was born!**

PSALM 139

Psalm 139 would have to be one of the most well-known of all Bible passages. It is written by King David, who reflects on God, praising Him for knowing everything, knowing us intimately and being everywhere. The following excerpt is from Psalm 139: 13–18 (NIV).

"For you formed my inward parts; you knitted me together in my mother's womb. I praise you, for I am fearfully and wonderfully made.

"Wonderful are your works; my soul knows it very well.

"My frame was not hidden from you, when I was being made in secret, intricately woven in the depths of the earth.

"Your eyes saw my unformed substance; in your book were written, every one of them, the days that were formed for me, when as yet there was none of them.

"How precious to me are your thoughts, O God! How vast is the sum of them! If I would count them, they are more than the sand."

What a great passage about the miracle of human conception and birth! David describes God as intricately weaving and embroidering a masterpiece in the mother's womb. He not only declares that God designed and formed us, but that He also planned, determined, and numbered our days before we had even set foot on this earth.

BEFORE YOU WERE BORN

Many other Bible passages talk about God knowing us *"before we were born"*. Whether God is talking about knowing us from the womb or before conception, it is not always clear. Regardless, the main thing to know is that He has had His hand on your life every single step of the way along your journey.

Here are some verses you may like to read:

- *"Before I formed you in the womb, I knew you, and before you were born I consecrated you; I appointed you a prophet to the nations."* (Jeremiah 1:5, ESV)

- *"Thus says the Lord who made you, who formed you from the womb and will help you: Fear not, O Jacob my servant, Jeshurun whom I have chosen."* (Isaiah 44:2, ESV)
- *"Listen to me, O coastlands, and give attention, you peoples from afar. The Lord called me from the womb, from the body of my mother he named my name."* (Isaiah 49:1, ESV)
- *"But when He who had set me apart before I was born, and who called me by His grace…"* (Galatians 1:15, ESV)
- *"Yet you are He who took me from the womb; you made me trust you at my mother's breasts. On you was I cast from my birth, and from my mother's womb you have been my God."* (Psalm 22:9–10, ESV)
- *"For we are his workmanship, created in Christ Jesus for good works, which God prepared beforehand, that we should walk in them."* (Ephesians 2:10, ESV)
- *"Blessed be the God and Father of our Lord Jesus Christ, who has blessed us in Christ with every spiritual blessing in the heavenly places, even as He chose us in Him before the foundation of the world, that we should be holy and blameless before Him."* (Ephesians 1:3–4, ESV)
- *"For you, O Lord, are my hope, my trust, O Lord, from my youth. Upon you I have leaned from before my birth; you are He who took me from my mother's womb. My praise is continually of you."* (Psalm 71:5–6, ESV)

RIGHT HERE, RIGHT NOW

If we believe that we have been created in the image of God; formed and knitted uniquely by Him, then we must also believe He has a plan and purpose for each of our lives. As you pray, thank God for creating you – His unique, marvellous work, made in His likeness. Pray that God will strengthen you to daily yield yourself to Him to walk in His plans and purpose for your life.

Influence

So now you know that your loving Creator God has predestined you and has prepared an exciting plan for your life, this is a good time to remember that you also have a free will to make choices. Here are a couple of Scriptures that talk about our ability to choose and how important it is to make the right choices in life.

"Now fear the Lord and serve him with all faithfulness. Throw away the gods your ancestors worshipped beyond the Euphrates River and in Egypt, and serve the Lord. But if serving the Lord seems undesirable to you, then **choose for yourselves this day whom you will serve**, *whether the gods your ancestors served beyond the Euphrates or the gods of the Amorites, in whose land you are living. But as for me and my household, we will serve the Lord."* (Joshua 24:14–15, NIV, emphasis added)

"This day I call the heavens and the earth as witnesses against you that I have set before you life and death, blessings and curses. Now **choose life**, *so that you and your children may live and that you may love the Lord your God, listen to his voice, and hold fast to him."*
(Deuteronomy 30:19–20, NIV, emphasis added)

Some choices (such as where to live, who to marry and what job to take) are major; while others (such as what to eat for breakfast) are small. Your life will comprise of a series of these types of decisions joined together. Therefore, you become a product of the decisions that you make – both for good or for bad.

The decisions you make propel you onward, and without decision, you will remain static and ineffectual. Your decisions are fuelled by your thoughts, opinions, knowledge, experiences, beliefs and con-science – all of which have been heavily influenced by the people and circumstances that flow in and out of your life.

Let's have a look at eight different types of influence that can radi-cally affect the decisions you make.

1 Parents or caregivers.
2 Family.
3 Friends and peers.
4 Teachers and people in authority.
5 Culture and society.
6 Your beliefs.
7 Opportunity.
8 Circumstance.

1 PARENTS AND CAREGIVERS

Parents and caregivers have been given a tremendous responsibility. We know that some parents perform their parental duty well, and oth-ers not so well. We also know that words are powerful (*"Death and life are in the power of the tongue."*, Proverbs 18:21, NKJV). Parents have the power to encourage a child in their gifts and passions or squash their dreams.

When I was 16 years old, I needed to select subjects for my final year of school. These subjects would be the springboard off which I would then move into a tertiary course and ultimately into a career.

My mother was an incredibly encouraging woman who took the parental approach of *"I'll support you no matter what you want to do"* (which was lovely and greatly appreciated). However, she wasn't the only parental-esque voice of influence in my life at that time; there was another close relative on the scene who had a rather commanding presence.

When I declared my love of art and creativity and my desire to pursue art-related subjects, my relative said something to me that I will never forget – he said: "*you'll never make money from art*". I listened to those words, made a 180° change, and chose all science subjects (my next favourite topic), leaving behind my love of art, photography and art history as 'useless' subjects that couldn't possibly lead to any respectable career (or so that person thought).

The problem was that I didn't perform well in those science subjects, and I did not enjoy that year of learning. Following the path that I had now carved for myself (following another's advice, but not my heart), I left school and embarked on a tertiary science course. My studies lasted a total of six months, at which point I ended up back at my high school, sitting in the office of the careers counsellor, crying because I hated my course and I had no idea what to do with my life.

The counsellor asked me a simple question, "*what did I enjoy doing?*", and I replied "*art*". These were pre-internet days, so we proceeded to work our way through her filing cabinet of leaflets and booklets and case studies of potential careers and courses, and we pulled out anything we could find to do with art or photography.

We came across the trade of 'photolithography', which is essentially what graphic design is today, but before computers came into the industry. The older brother of my first boyfriend was an apprentice photolithographer. I remembered when he showed me two images of a tall ship anchored in a lagoon. One picture looked like paradise, with a beautiful blue sky and sparkling water, the other image contrasted with a cloudy sky and dull-coloured water. I remember how fascinated I was with this image transformation, and this single encounter with photolithography was the catalyst to send me on my new career path.

I told my high school counsellor that photolithography was the one, so she encouraged me to write letters of introduction to a handful of prospective employers, asking for an apprenticeship. One replied with a "*yes*", and the rest is (my) history. And guess what? Pretty soon I was 'making money' from (a form of) 'art'. God ultimately got me back on the right path for my life. Perhaps, if I had not been swayed by a voice of influence, and listened to my heart and gut (telling me what I knew I loved to do), my journey would have been a little quicker.

Parents, please don't be a wet blanket on the 'fire' of your child's life – fan the flames! You will inevitably have a profound influence on your children and their ideas. Even if your child ends up changing the direction of their career or life, be the person who they remember as the one who stood by and encouraged them when they needed your support.

It's super-important to observe your children (from a very young age) and encourage their interests. God has created each of us (every adult and child) as unique and special individuals, our own unique set of gifts and abilities. These don't just magically appear as an adult; they are within us all of our lives.

But, remember, there is a fine line between encouraging a child and forcing them. As long as you allow your children to try new things (and be OK with it if they decide an activity is not for them); and then encourage and support them as much as possible, then that's your job well done.

2 FAMILY

Often we embrace the passions of our family due to their enthusiasm and encouragement. For example, if you have an outdoor-loving family, the chances are high that you will enjoy the outdoors as much as your family does.

Sometimes the opposite is also true. Both my father and mother were pattern makers and tailors within the fashion industry, and my father established a clothing manufacturing business. He died when I was a baby, and his clothing business passed to my half-brother, yet – thanks to my mother – I still grew up in and around fashion, fabric and sewing machines.

My mother taught me to sew from a very young age. However, while I was able to understand the mechanics of sewing and loved being around colourful fabrics, beads and buttons, I did not embrace a love for sewing in the way that my mother did. Sewing and fashion were never to be my path as they were for her.

God knew what He was doing when he put you in the family that He did. Sometimes our family experiences will mould and shape us; strengthen us; teach us or warn us, and sometimes they will educate and equip us for the road ahead. While your family can and will have a tremendous influence on your life, they should never define who you are.

3 FRIENDS AND PEERS

American entrepreneur, author and motivational speaker, Jim Rohn, said: *"You're the average of the five people you spend most of your time with."* Now that's a challenging thought!

Think about the five people who you spent most of your time with (1) as a young child; (2) as a teenager, and (3) as an adult. How did their opinions and actions influence your opinions and actions? Did they influence your life path in any way? How? Was their influence positive or negative? Would you go back and change anything if you could?

My three best friends in high school were a massive influence on my life. They were (and are) amazing humans – sporty, clean-living and super-intelligent. They didn't smoke, do drugs or party. They studied hard and achieved some of the best grades in school, and all went on to become exceptional adults with families of their own.

We were all different, with different world views, religious beliefs and personal opinions. Still, our common interests and personalities drew us together and informed how we would interact and what we would do as a group of friends.

I thank God that I had the friends that I did and made the choices I made. To this day, I have never smoked a cigarette or taken drugs, and I have never consumed so much alcohol that I had a hangover the next day. My story may have been quite different had I chosen to associate with another circle of friends.

I do not doubt that my entry into adulthood was strongly informed by the influence that my friends had on me as a teenager. Their friendship didn't specifically dictate my path in terms of interests and career direction, but they did influence my attitude, determination, outlook on life and desire to succeed.

Who do you spend most of your time with now? What words are they speaking into your life? What examples are they setting for you (and, by default, the people around you)? It might be time to have a rethink about where and with whom you are investing your time.

Also, be wary of the nay-sayers in your circle of friends and acquaintances. These are people who can crush your dreams or ideas with their words or actions. They are people who may think they are offering wise counsel, but who base their opinions on their own biases and experiences rather than with an understanding of God's Word and what He is doing in your life.

4 TEACHERS AND PEOPLE IN AUTHORITY

Swimming has never been a strength of mine, and I am OK to admit that (plus it's always handy to know one's limitations). When I was two years old, my mother took me to swim classes, and from the moment the instructor dunked my head under the water (and held it there, so Mum said) I decided that swimming wasn't for me.

Fast forward to 1984 and 12-year-old me has just finished an assessment for a life-saving certificate. My school required every student to swim a certain number of laps to get their award. My version of swimming was to flap around a bit, then stand up and take a breath, then flap around a bit more, and eventually, I would make it to the other side.

There I was, dripping wet at the side of the pool, waiting for my teacher to give me my results. She looked at me, and said (and I quote)

"You're useless, you'll never be any good." That was it, word-for-word, emblazoned into my memory for the next 40 years.

That teacher had the power to make or break me as a swimmer. She could have been encouraging or helped to teach me the skills to improve myself, but she decided to break me with her words. You know what? I proved her half-wrong. As a teenager I joined the school underwater hockey team and (armed with the assistance of mask, snorkel and flippers) I performed reasonably well; and as an adult, I love to go snorkelling. So, swimming wasn't going to be my wheelhouse or my joy, and that's OK. What wasn't OK was the negative influence that teacher left on my spirit.

On the flip side, there are also outstanding, impactful, inspiring teachers in this world who can and do influence for good.

We all spend a significant portion of our earthly existence under the influence of people in authority, in places such as educational institutions, jobs or churches. We often listen to the same person (or people) speak to us for weeks, months or even years at a time, and that is a lot of influence that we allow (or are forced to accept) into our lives. These voices can inspire and uplift or tear us down. They can open our minds to new possibilities or distract you from your path. Be wise and wary as you listen to the many voices in your life (including those of other Believers), especially those people in authority over you.

5 CULTURE AND SOCIETY

In 2010 a very special Christmas card arrived from a young girl named Djeneba, a World Vision child that my husband and I sponsored in Mali, Africa. She was 8 years old at the time, and most of the correspondence that we received would have a hand-drawn picture or a letter, but this card was different. This card had a hand print, and it was the hand print that made me cry.

From that print, you could not tell if the person was male or female, the country they came from, the language they spoke, their age or their ethnicity. They were simply a child, like any other child, anywhere in the world – a remarkable human being created by God.

It just so happened that this particular child was born into poverty in a land affected by economic hardship, famine and war; and into a religious mix of Islam, Dogon and Christianity.

Will the cultural pressures and expectations that Djeneba was born into influence her life and path? Yes, of course. There is no doubt that our culture and society have a considerable impact on the direction our life and purpose will take.

Djeneba's culture is figuratively, literally and physically a world apart from my culture. The society that surrounds her – education, opportunities, finances, health, welfare, religion and familial expectations are totally different from mine. Will she be able to walk in her God-given gifts and purpose in the same way that I can? Absolutely!

God knew exactly where Djeneba would be born, when she would be born, and the culture she would be born into. He planted her there for a reason, to make an impact on HER world and sphere of influence. God planted me in New Zealand to make an impact on MY world and my sphere of influence. We all have a part to play, no matter our cultural background, or the life we were born into.

6 YOUR BELIEFS

Science has long-proven that the mind (including your thoughts and your beliefs) is a powerful thing and can have a strong influence on the way you choose to live.

One of the most basic ways that beliefs can shape your reality is through their influence on your behaviour. For example, if you believe that you're capable, competent, and deserving of your dream job, you're probably more likely to notice and seek out opportunities that could help you get there. If you believe that you are not worthy of recognition, then that will come across in your job interviews and social interactions and could jeopardise your opportunities and relationships.

Beliefs can also influence health behaviours. People are more likely to engage in healthy behaviours (like eating well and exercising) if they believe that they are capable of effectively performing these tasks.

Beliefs about your basic character – who you are as a person on a fundamental level – can be especially powerful. For example, research suggests that while guilt (feeling that you did a bad thing) can motivate self-improvement, shame (feeling like you are a bad person) tends to create a self-fulfilling prophecy, reducing hope and undermining efforts to change.

Then you have your spiritual (some people would say 'religious') beliefs which shape how you think about God, the Bible, salvation, life after death, and so on. Spiritual beliefs impact human behaviour in every aspect of our lives by us wanting to (or having to) live by the codes, morals and rules of the religion that we choose to follow. Even atheism is a form of belief – a belief that there is no God or gods. Whether you follow a religion or not, you are forming a belief system that will guide your life in various ways.

This complex belief system will be unique to you and will permeate every single facet of your existence. The system will be developed throughout your life, and be contributed to by your parents; your family; the people around you; your church; TV and movies; the media; literature and countless other voices.

What you believe, how you think about yourself and how you think about others all have a heavy influence on how you make choices and the quality of those choices.

As you know, this book is heavily biased toward those who follow a Christian belief system or have a Christian world view (which is another way of thinking about beliefs). Therefore, I'm going to suggest that the best way to do a health check on your beliefs is to use the Bible as your benchmark. Always ask yourself, what would the Bible say about this or that.

There are very few topics that the Bible does not cover, but if you do find the odd one or two, then I'm confident that you'll discover the relevant principles, behaviours and attitudes behind the topic will be in there for you to search out.

7 OPPORTUNITY

Growing up, my mother and I did not have much money to spare, but somehow my mother used to put aside enough funds to send me to holiday and after-school classes and workshops. I would eagerly look forward to receiving (via snail mail in those days) notice of these classes. As a pre-teen, I would scour each page and highlight the courses that appealed to me.

I remember doing classes in painting, drawing, puppet making, pottery, etching, jazz ballet, tap dancing, guitar and speech and drama. Some classes I loved, some I did not. I remember going to only one or two tap dancing and speech and drama classes before saying to Mum that I did not want to go back. To her credit, my mother never once made me feel bad about not continuing. She didn't tell me that I had wasted her money, or that I didn't have stickability. She – bless every bone in her body – would say *"I'm happy if you're happy"*. She said that to me my whole life and made sure I knew that she was there to support my choices, even if she disagreed with them.

Though my mother could not buy me the 'fine' things in life, she bought me the opportunity to experiment and explore, and for that, I will be forever grateful. Even to this day, if I think of a new activity that I would like to try, I'll book myself into a workshop to give it a go. You are never, ever too old to try something new, and you never know where your explorations may take you or who you might meet along the way.

Sometimes we have to put ourselves out there and create opportunities to experience new things (rather than wait for opportunities to come to us). When I was 18 years old, I decided to become a Campus Life leader, which I did for three years. Campus Life was a Youth For Christ programme for high school-age youth. We would meet together weekly to tackle teen-related topics in a fun and impactful way from a Christian perspective, and every so often we would take the teens on camps and outdoor activities. We would tell the young folk that participation in the activities was 'challenge by choice'. We would give each person the opportunity to take part, but would never berate or belittle them if they chose not to get involved. The only thing was, as a leader, I had to lead by example!

My decision to be a youth leader meant that I, too, was exposed to activities that I may never have had the chance to experience otherwise. Through this leadership commitment, I was able to try things like bush hiking, abseiling, canoeing, rafting, skiing, horse riding, windsurfing, karting, acting, singing and making videos.

I am convinced that many of the skills I acquired during this time became the foundation of my path to come – especially in the areas of confidence, group leadership, public speaking, activity planning, and my 'no fear' and 'give it a go' approach to life.

Never underestimate the value in joining a group – no matter your age. The group could be Scouts or Girl Guides; a church youth group; interest group; sports team; outdoor pursuits club; craft guild or humanitarian group. The choices are as endless as there are interests. Remember, how will you know if you like something unless you give it a go?!

8 CIRCUMSTANCE

Will the child from a wealthy family, who has the best private school education, the widest opportunities, or most influential family connections have a better chance of finding their life path? The good news is no – not at all.

We will see – through our 12 Steps to finding your God-given purpose – that your profession and how you can monetise your skills become part of the purpose-equation. However, your purpose is not determined by your bank account (or your parents' bank account), past, present or future.

Money can undoubtedly open doors and create opportunities, but money cannot buy your passions, your talents or your gifts.

Think for a moment about a woman by the name of Agnes Gonxha Bojaxhiu, who later came to be known as Mother Theresa.

Agnes was born in 1910 in the Republic of Macedonia to Nikola, who owned a successful construction business, and Drana - mother to three of five surviving children. They were a devout Catholic family. In 1919, at age 9 years old, Agnes's father, Nikola, died and her privileged life changed overnight.

From a young age, Agnes felt a calling to be a nun and serve by helping the poor. At the age of 18, she was given permission to join a group of nuns in Ireland. After a few months of training, with the Sisters of Loreto, she was then permitted to travel to India. She took her formal religious vows in 1931 and chose to be named after St Therese of Lisieux – the patron saint of missionaries. Theresa based her service on the fundamental principle of the teachings of Jesus Christ, and her mission was to look after people who nobody else was willing to care for.

The rest of Mother Theresa's story has been well-written into our history books, and her humanitarian works would go on to inspire people around the globe.

Mother Theresa knew her purpose in life, without a shadow of a doubt. She was determined, focused and courageous. She and her fellow nuns survived on minimal income and food, often having to beg for funds. Money would ultimately help to support and extend her missionary activity, but it was only a means to an end. If you took the money away, her purpose and 'fire' to make a difference remained, irrespective of her circumstances.

SILENCING THE VOICES

Have you been greatly affected or influenced by the myriad of voices in your life? Have you been left wondering who you are and how you fit in? You are not alone.

By allowing the world (and all those influencing factors) to validate or inform who you are can only leave you confused. It's not until you can see your identity through God's eyes that understanding who you are begins to make sense.

One thing you can know for sure is that the Bible says – over and over again – how much you are loved, wanted, and carefully-created.

Also, the Bible promises that those who seek God; acknowledge what Jesus Christ did for them at the cross of Calvary; turn from their sinful ways and follow Him, will be embraced as a child of God. So, who are you? You are a child of God. Wow! I don't know about you, but I find that rather phenomenal.

Many Bible verses help us to understand the way that God looks at us. Here are two of them:

- *"For those who are led by the Spirit of God are the children of God. The Spirit you received does not make you slaves so that you live in fear again; rather, the Spirit you received brought about your adoption to sonship. And by Him, we cry, "Abba, Father." The Spirit himself testifies with our spirit that we are God's children. Now if we are children, then we are heirs – heirs of God and co-heirs with Christ, if indeed*

we share in his sufferings in order that we may also share in his glory." (Romans 8:14–17, NIV)
- *"Yet to all who did receive Him, to those who believed in His name, He gave the right to become children of God – children born not of natural descent, not of human decision or a husband's will, but born of God."* (John 1:12–13, NIV)

No matter what has been spoken over your life, and no matter who you currently believe you are, you have a precious spiritual heritage behind you; an exciting future in front of you, and you are 100% loved. There is a specific reason that you are on this planet, and I know this because I know – without a doubt – that God does not make mistakes.

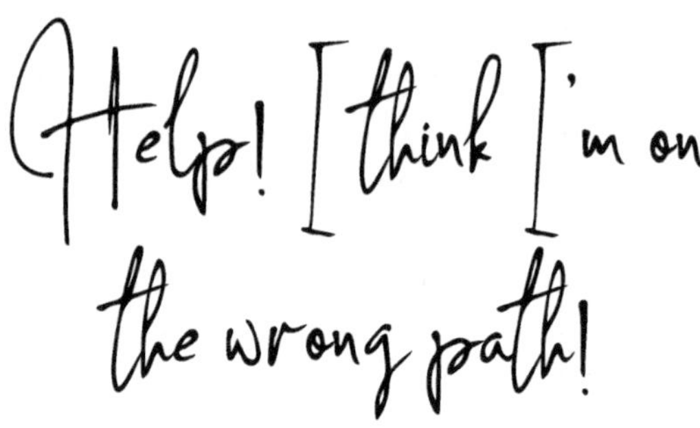

"The Devil has a plot, but God has a plan."
(John Ramirez)

Have you ever had that sinking feeling like you've made a wrong decision (or a series of wrong decisions) and that your life-path has gone off-course? That was me in 1993, at 21 years of age, when I made a conscious choice to marry my first husband.

Funnily enough, I knew from the day after the wedding that I had made the wrong move, but – by then – I thought it was too late, that I'd have to tough it out, and that things would get better over time. Things didn't get better, and six years later, we separated.

WHY DID GOD 'LET' ME MAKE SUCH A WRONG DECISION?

In the Bible (in 1 Samuel 8) the elders of Israel gathered together and demanded that the prophet Samuel ask God to give them a king *"such as all other nations have"*.

God had always intended for Israel to have a king, but it had to be the right person at the right time with the right qualifications. It had been written (long before) in Deuteronomy 17:15 where God said: "… *be sure to appoint over you a king the Lord your God chooses.*" However, the elders were impatient and sought to bring about a king at a time of their choosing, not in God's time.

The people made their request, and – though it displeased Him – God gave them Saul when they should have waited patiently for David. In the end, God did appoint David as King, though the road to his kingship was perhaps not as smooth as it may have been had the people not tried to force God's hand.

So, why did God 'let' me make such a fateful decision with my first marriage? Because I willed it. I chose it. I requested it like the Israelites requested Saul. I wanted what 'other nations' (or, in my case, other people) had – a wedding, a home of my own and a chance for independence. I made the choice without consulting God (or at least without waiting for His answer). I was headstrong and thought I knew what was best for my life.

As a king, Saul disobeyed God, and so God withdrew his favour from Saul's life. I felt the same way, that I was living a life devoid of favour and one that I was sure God had not chosen for me.

WHAT THE WRONG PATH LOOKS LIKE

If your pathway has become out of sync with God's purposes and plans, you'll know it. You'll see it and feel it. Each person will be different, but here are some signs that you are living outside of God's ideal for your life.

You'll feel:
- Out of sync with God.
- 'Stuck'.
- Like you are on the hamster wheel of life; never getting anywhere; a broken record; in a rut.

- No joy.
- No excitement.
- No sense of purpose or direction; listless; wandering.
- No sense of fulfilment.
- Like a failure.
- No sense of 'rightness'.
- A loss of identity.
- Like you are not using your gifts.

One of the most tell-tale signs is that there will be a lack of fruitfulness in your life. Let's take a look at a passage in the Bible which talks about 'spiritual fruit' (Galatians 5:13–26, NIV).

"You, my brothers and sisters, were called to be free. But do not use your freedom to indulge the flesh; rather, serve one another humbly in love. For the entire law is fulfilled in keeping this one command: "Love your neighbour as yourself." If you bite and devour each other, watch out or you will be destroyed by each other.

"So I say, walk by the Spirit, and you will not gratify the desires of the flesh. For the flesh desires what is contrary to the Spirit, and the Spirit what is contrary to the flesh. They are in conflict with each other, so that you are not to do whatever you want. But if you are led by the Spirit, you are not under the law.

"The acts of the flesh are obvious: sexual immorality, impurity and debauchery; idolatry and witchcraft; hatred, discord, jealousy, fits of rage, selfish ambition, dissensions, factions and envy; drunkenness, orgies, and the like. I warn you, as I did before, that those who live like this will not inherit the kingdom of God.

"But the fruit of the Spirit is love, joy, peace, forbearance [patience], kindness, goodness, faithfulness, gentleness and self-control. Against such things, there is no law. Those who belong to Christ Jesus have crucified the flesh with its passions and desires. Since we live by the Spirit, let us keep in step with the Spirit. Let us not become conceited, provoking and envying each other."

What type of fruit are you producing in your life? Good fruit; much fruit; lasting fruit? Are you making a difference in the lives of others? Now would be a great time to do a health-check on your spiritual orchard. It may be that some pruning or fertilising is required.

GETTING BACK ON TRACK

I've always believed that every life experience – whether good or bad – is valuable. Every crummy job; every frog that you kissed hoping it would turn into a prince (or princess); every mistake made. The times when you were barely treading water, or even going backwards, were also times where you were learning, growing and preparing for things to bloom.

God taught me many lessons during my first marriage and in the months after our separation. Life during this time wasn't all bad, and I know that many of my experiences have formed some of the building blocks for how my God-given purpose outworks today, 30 years later. God can turn the worst times in our lives around for the ultimate good.

With God's help, I was able to recover from the epic failure of my first marriage; gradually piece my life back together, and adjust my path as I returned my focus to Him. I realised just how far I had moved away from living a Bible-believing, Spirit-led life, and this was the time for a reset.

I sometimes joke that I missed out on my 20s, and that it was my 'lost decade'. The amazing thing is that God is a redeemer; He can take what is broken and make it whole again. In Joel 2:25–26 (NIV) it is written: "*I will repay you for the years the locusts have eaten…you will have plenty to eat, until you are full, and you will praise the name of the Lord your God, who has worked wonders for you…*" God has most certainly made up for the 'locust' years of my 20s.

Eventually, God brought my second husband – Simon – into my life. I can't say that I should have waited for Simon (in the same way that the Israelites should have waited for David), but what I do know is that he was the right husband for me at the right time. Together we have built a marriage that is godly with a solid biblical foundation. Out of that obedience has come the fruit of a life lived in God's purpose.

I know what it feels like to live both inside and outside of God's plan, and I have 100% certainty which path I prefer to walk on.

Here are some tips for getting yourself back in alignment with God's purpose for your life:

- **Be willing to change.** Getting back on track may only require small tweaks, or it may take a major overhaul. You need to be willing and determined to make whatever change is required, no matter what that change entails.
- **Surround yourself with godly and God-minded people** who will understand and encourage you and your gifts, not squash them.
- **Build spiritual muscle.** Get match-fit for life through prayer and reading the Bible.
- **Ask God for a new direction.** Once you acknowledge you've deviated off your path, ask God to help you find your way again.
- **Take time out.** Have one-on-one time with God – to think, reflect and have a good chat about next steps.
- **Fix the holes in your net.** Small holes become large holes under pressure. Are there areas of your life where you are exposed, or are dropping the spiritual ball, or are open for Satan to take a jab at you? Best deal to them before your net tears and the fish fall out.
- **Catch the little foxes.** "*Catch for us the foxes, the little foxes that ruin the vineyards, our vineyards that are in bloom.*" (Song of Solomon 2:15, NIV). Foxes are an analogy of potential problems. Can you see any little foxes in your life that need addressing?
- **Find a new perspective.** Start looking at your life and journey through God's eyes rather than your own eyes (or the eyes of others). The view is way better that way!
- **Be on the watch.** God will bring people and opportunities across your path. Be observant so you can recognise, then maximise each interaction.
- **Trust God.** He knows what is best for you.

Moses

A book about purpose would not be complete without looking at the life of Moses. Through Moses' birth, upbringing and experiences, we have been given a fabulous example of how purpose outworks throughout a person's life, from birth to death.

MOSES THROUGH THE EYES OF STEPHEN

You can read all about Moses in the book of Exodus (in the Bible). That's a lot of reading, so – to save you some time – there is a summary of Moses' life in the book of Acts, given to us by one of the earliest members of the Christian church, Stephen.

Stephen lived in Jerusalem at the time of Jesus Christ and became a follower of Jesus' teaching. He was one of seven men who the apostles chose to distribute food to widows in the early church, and the Bible records that he was *"full of God's grace and power,* [who] *performed great wonders and signs among the people."* (Acts 6:8. NIV).

Stephen's display of his faith led to him being falsely accused of blasphemy and brought before the Sanhedrin (the supreme council and tribunal of the Jews) to answer for his actions.

Stephen was given the opportunity to defend himself; instead, he used his time to talk about God, the mighty works God had done, and how people and events in history had pointed to Jesus Christ, the son of God. He accused Israel of their failure to recognise Jesus as their

Messiah (instead, rejecting and murdering Him). These accusations enraged his Jewish audience, and he was taken out of the city and stoned to death, making Stephen the first Christian martyr.

Acts 7 is the record of Stephen's remarkable testimony, which is also a detailed and concise history of Israel (the Jews) and their relationship to God.

In Acts 7:17–53 (NIV), Stephen gives us a helpful overview of Moses' life, which we will unpack further as we work our way through *Purpose Made*.

"As the time drew near for God to fulfil his promise to Abraham, the number of our people in Egypt had greatly increased. Then a new king, to whom Joseph meant nothing, came to power in Egypt. He dealt treacherously with our people and oppressed our ancestors by forcing them to throw out their newborn babies so that they would die.

"At that time, Moses was born, and he was no ordinary child. For three months he was cared for by his family. When he was placed outside, Pharaoh's daughter took him and brought him up as her own son. Moses was educated in all the wisdom of the Egyptians and was powerful in speech and action.

"When Moses was forty years old, he decided to visit his own people, the Israelites. He saw one of them being mistreated by an Egyptian, so he went to his defence and avenged him by killing the Egyptian. Moses thought that his own people would realise that God was using him to rescue them, but they did not. The next day Moses came upon two Israelites who were fighting. He tried to reconcile them by saying, 'Men, you are brothers; why do you want to hurt each other?'

"But the man who was mistreating the other pushed Moses aside and said, 'Who made you ruler and judge over us? Are you thinking of killing me as you killed the Egyptian yesterday?' When Moses heard this, he fled to Midian, where he settled as a foreigner and had two sons.

"After forty years had passed, an angel appeared to Moses in the flames of a burning bush in the desert near Mount Sinai. When he saw this, he was amazed at the sight. As he went over to get a closer look, he heard the Lord

say: 'I am the God of your fathers, the God of Abraham, Isaac and Jacob.' Moses trembled with fear and did not dare to look.

"Then the Lord said to him, 'Take off your sandals, for the place where you are standing is holy ground. I have indeed seen the oppression of my people in Egypt. I have heard their groaning and have come down to set them free. Now come, I will send you back to Egypt.'

"This is the same Moses they had rejected with the words, 'Who made you ruler and judge?' He was sent to be their ruler and deliverer by God himself, through the angel who appeared to him in the bush. He led them out of Egypt and performed wonders and signs in Egypt, at the Red Sea and for forty years in the wilderness."

THREE BLOCKS OF 40 YEARS

That was a very short summary of Moses' very long life (120 years)! We can break up those 120 years into three distinct blocks of 40 years.

BLOCK #1

Moses' first 40 years were spent as a prince of Egypt, living as the grandson of the king (Pharaoh). Moses was actually born into a Hebrew family, but when Pharaoh ordered that all Hebrew baby boys be slaughtered at birth, Moses' mother set her son adrift on the River Nile in a basket made of rushes to save his life. His basket was spotted by the daughter of the Pharaoh of Egypt, who adopted the child and raised him as Egyptian royalty.

Moses knew he was born of Hebrew parents, and he would have known his story and the story of his people which meant that Moses was straddling two worlds.

Moses was keenly aware of the hardship and injustice that Pharaoh was inflicting on the Hebrew people (his people). By killing the Egyptian, he was presumptive and took vengeance into his own hands, rather than allowing God to move at the appointed time.

The Bible says that Moses was *"powerful in speech and action"*. For his first 40 years, Moses would likely have been operating in his own strength, backed by the security and might of the Egyptian palace.

From what we read, Moses had a heart for his people and an inkling of God's purpose for his life. He probably felt he was chosen to deliver the Hebrews, but he acted too soon, and his own people did not receive him. He was a reconciler with misplaced confidence in himself. After he murdered the Egyptian, he must have had a revelation that God was not going to vindicate him, and so he fled from the palace to the desert.

BLOCK #2

Moses' second 40 years (40 to 80 years old) were spent in Midian (modern-day Saudi Arabia) living as the son-in-law of Jethro, the priest of Midian, and tending Jethro's flocks. What a change of role, from a prince of Egypt to a shepherd! During this time he married Zipporah and had two sons, Gershom and Eliezer.

This was Moses' period of humbling – from the time he fled the palace, he had to wait another 40 years to receive a complete revelation from God about his purpose and assignment. Perhaps his 'Midian years' were a time for his impulsive personality to be moulded; to learn to live a life of simplicity and humility, and to develop his respect for God.

BLOCK #3

His third 40 years (80 to 120 years old) would give Moses the biggest challenge of his life. To begin with, Moses was told – by God – to return to Egypt to see Pharaoh (back into the palace where he grew up but left in disgrace 40 years earlier) and ask him to let the Hebrew people go.

God was allowing Moses to do what he thought he would do all those years before – help to deliver his people out of bondage in Egypt. It was as if God was saying, "*In spite of what has gone before, I still choose you. It's now time for you to do what you were born to do*".

Exodus 4–12 is a record of the interchange between Moses, his brother (Aaron), and Pharaoh, and the famous ten plagues that God sent on the Egyptians until Pharaoh finally granted Moses' request.

Along with Aaron, Moses guided *"about six hundred thousand men on foot, besides women and children"* out of Egypt (Exodus 12:37, NIV) and through the Red Sea, which God miraculously parted. He led this multitude through the wilderness of what is modern-day Egypt, Saudi Arabia, Jordan and Israel, as they journeyed for 40 years together to their ultimate destination of the Promised Land (Israel).

SUPERNATURAL PROVISION

Can you imagine the level of responsibility and expectations that God laid on Moses, and how Moses must have felt? From the time that God first spoke to Moses through the burning bush (Exodus 3), He promised Moses that He would be with him every step of the way – and God never once let Moses or the Israelites down. In fact, the Bible tells us that Moses and God had an extraordinary relationship where *"the Lord would speak to Moses face-to-face, as one speaks to a friend."* (Exodus 33:11, NIV). That's what I call supernatural reassurance!

God gave Moses everything he needed, at just the right time – assistance; words to say; directions; food and water; wisdom and knowledge. I couldn't imagine anyone being given a greater calling and assignment, and whenever Moses pressed into God, He was always there.

Whatever level of calling and assignments that God gives you, He will be faithful to help you achieve it. We can look at the example of Moses and take courage – God gives us these examples to build our faith and to set precedents. If He has done it before, He can do it again. That means if He calls you to do anything (be it small or great), then He will give you all you need to fulfil the task and He will remain with you every step of the way.

"Your body could rule you, and your mind could rule you, but your spirit is supposed to rule you. We are born again, we are new creatures, and that's where God speaks to us – in the spirit, in our spirit. He's spirit; He speaks spirit-to-spirit. That's the key. There are so many voices out there, right now, but there is only one that we need to hear, and that's the Commander of our faith [Jesus Christ]. That's our Father, that is the Holy Spirit who has been sent. All three of those are talking to us because they are in us."
(Kevin Zadai, SidRoth.org, 9 August 2020)

When it comes to outworking God's purpose for your life it's super-important that you clearly and correctly understand what your gifts, calling and assignments are and know what God expects you to do with that knowledge. To do that, you first need to hear what He is saying to you so you can then obediently follow through. Easier said than done, right?!

Christians talk a lot about 'hearing from God' or 'hearing the voice of God'. I've been a Bible-believing Christian for 40+ years, and – for most of that time – I despaired that I didn't know how to recognise God's voice. As a consequence, I was never 100% sure that any of my undertakings were part of God's plan for my life. All I was doing, throughout that time, was making sure that my actions and intentions were biblically sound (e.g. in line with God's Word), and relying on doors to providentially open and close when required. The concept was admirable, yet I was woefully deficient in my understanding of how God operates.

I know now that God speaks to me via what I can only describe to others as a 'download', and that He's been speaking to me this way since my teenage years.

The time when I usually receive these 'downloads' is just before I fall asleep or just as I am waking up when my spirit is peaceful, and my head is clear. I'm usually a very sound sleeper, but sometimes I will also awake during the night and cannot get back to sleep, and I'll ask God if He wants to tell me something. I keep paper and a pen beside my bed to be ready at any time.

This 'download' is more than just getting a random 'idea' popping into my head, it's a stream of thought accompanied by a sense of 'urgency' or 'compulsion' to write those thoughts down on paper – and it usually amounts to pages and pages of words.

When I look back to when I was a teenager, I remember that I always kept a pen beside the bed. Sometimes I'd find that I didn't have any paper to write on, so I would end up writing on my arm (and would then have to decipher what I'd written in the morning).

Interestingly, God has chosen to speak to me in a way that aligns with my passion and calling for the written word – a method with which I resonate strongly.

The other fascinating (and perplexing) thing is that if God has been speaking to me this way for at least 25 years, how did I not recognise it earlier? When I would talk about my thoughts with others, I would usually say something like *"I've had an idea…"*. I can now see that many of these 'ideas' were not my ideas at all, but God's (whoops!).

The good thing is that now I know His particular method for me, I am more attuned to receiving messages and being able to discern if the words are from God or my own thoughts. My big challenge is that my brain tends to race around at 100 miles an hour, leaving very few quiet or still moments. Therefore, the onus falls on me to ensure that I give God the space He needs to communicate.

HEARING GOD'S VOICE

There are many, many ways in which God will speak to His children, and each person will hear from God in the way that's right for them. There are no right or wrong methods, as long as we are getting the right message at the right time. These various ways can include:

- Audible voice (Genesis 3:8, Exodus 20:1–22, 1 Samuel 3, Acts 9:3–7).
- Angels (Luke 1:26–38).
- Circumstances (Revelation 3:8).
- Coincidences.
- Conscience.
- Conversations (Romans 1:11–12).
- Animals (Numbers 22:28).
- Creation (Psalm 19:1–2, Romans 1:20, Matthew 6:26).
- Dreams (Daniel 2:19).
- The Holy Spirit (John 14:17, 1 Corinthians 3:16).
- Jesus Christ (Hebrews 1:1–2).
- Miracles.
- Music (2 Chronicles 20:21).
- Other Believers (including teachings, books, podcasts, videos, articles, movies, etc.) (1 Peter 4:11).
- Prayer (Jeremiah 33:3, Matthew 6:6, James 1:5, Romans 8:26–27), or a combination of prayer and fasting.
- Prophecy and prophetic words from others (1 Corinthians 14:31).
- Promptings.
- Restful times (Psalm 46:10).
- Signs (Judges 6:36–40).
- Spiritual happenings (Numbers 17:2–8).

- Still small voice (1 Kings 19:11–13, Romans 8:14–16).
- Thoughts and impressions (1 Corinthians 12:10).
- Visions (Acts 2:17–18).
- The Word – the Bible (Matthew 6:11).
- The Word – a living, rhema word (John 6:63).

Regardless of the way God chooses to reveal Himself or 'speak' to you, if you are in any doubt, line up what you hear against what you read in God's Word (the Bible). God will never tell you to do, think or say anything contrary to his Word. For example, He will never tell you to refuse to forgive someone or spend money frivolously. Everything that He tells you to do is designed to bring blessing into your life and minister grace to you.

God trains us to recognise His voice through His written Word. He uses it to tune our spiritual ears to what is real so that we can easily spot a counterfeit. When you're trained to hear God's voice through His Word, Satan will be unable to sneak deceptions in on you, and if Satan did try to deceive you with a religious-sounding voice, you would know not to believe it.

To live in confidence that you are hearing from Him, you need to hold His Word continually in your heart, and you do this by drawing near to God (James 4:8). God's not going to chase you, it's your responsibility to seek Him diligently, and that involves spending time in the Word and in prayer.

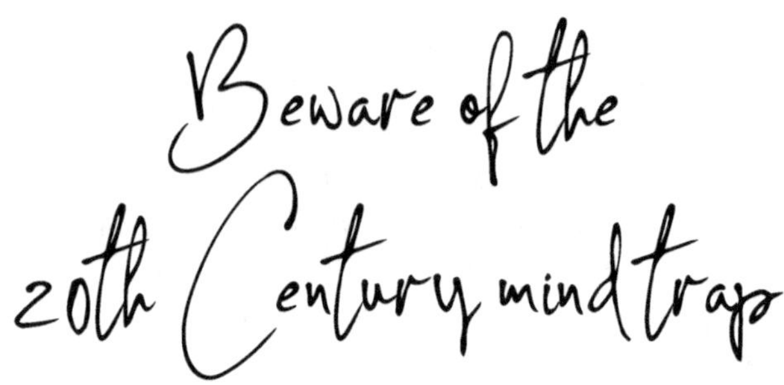

Beware of the 20th Century mindtrap

Have you ever heard yourself or someone else saying to a child, "little Johnny (or Jackie), when you grow up, you can be anything you want to be if you just work hard at it. The sky's the limit. Whatever you set your mind to do, you will do it."? Sound familiar?

This saying may well have been around since Adam, but it's been noticeably loud since the 1960s and the rise of global movements such as women's liberation, racial equality and humankind being able to do seemingly-impossible things such as set foot on the moon.

The notion that we <u>can</u> do anything that we want to do is a noble one – that all men, women, boys and girls should have equal opportunity to pursue their dreams regardless of gender, age, ethnicity and so on.

Looking at the statement through a purpose-lens, we need to question whether we <u>should</u> pursue certain things – or perhaps how we pursue certain things.

Let's use the example of a boy growing up who is mad keen on basketball. As a child, he practised drills and skills every day. He had a hoop set up at home and dedicated his daylight hours to the sport he loved. As the years ticked by, the boy continued his love of basketball, dreaming of one day playing in the NBA. He captained his high school team and won a basketball scholarship to a top college. But when it came to making the cut for the NBA, he fell short. After three years of trying, he gave up his NBA dream.

Did God predestine this boy to play in the NBA? It seems not. Is basketball meant to be part of that boy's God-given purpose? Perhaps. Perhaps he is destined to run a basketball programme for underprivileged kids. Perhaps he will train as a physical education teacher where he can share his love of basketball and other sports with the next generation. Perhaps basketball will only ever remain a pastime that he enjoyed for that period of his life.

I encourage you to recognise your God-given talents and develop them but leave yourself open as to where and how God is leading you. Hold your dreams lightly, so that if God asks you to change direction, you'll be able to do so with a malleable and joyful heart.

Beware of the 20th Century mind trap that is the phrase "you can be anything you want to be". Perhaps it's better to say "God has the perfect plan for you. Let's explore all the things you love to do and see where God leads."

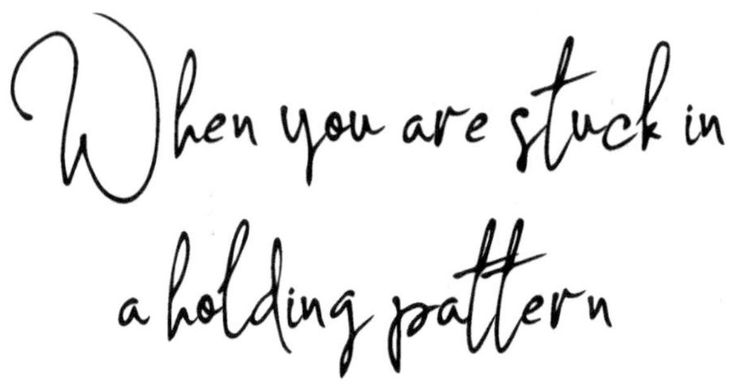

---

*"Appreciate where you are in your journey, even if it's not
where you want to be. Every season serves a purpose."* (Anon)

What happens if you understand your God-given gifts, and you've found some clarity around your purpose, but you are still feeling lost?

When an airplane approaches a runway, but has not yet been granted permission to land, ground control will often request that the plane fly around and around in a 'holding pattern' until a runway becomes available. Do you feel like you are stuck in a human 'holding pattern', waiting for the outworking of your purpose to kick off or resume?

Maybe you are currently working in a job that brings you no joy or sense of fulfilment. Maybe you can recognise your gifts and purpose, but no-one else seems to agree, or you lack support from friends and family. Spending time in a holding pattern (especially when you are chomping at the bit to do something constructive) can be frustrating, to say the least. I'm here to tell you that you are not alone, and you are in the company of some of the greatest biblical saints of all time.

Peter Mortlock (City Impact Church, New Zealand), gives us some insight into the life of Joseph, whom we can read about in Genesis 37–50. Joseph would have felt like he was stuck in a 'holding pattern' for literally years, but – thankfully – God knew the big picture for his life: "*Joseph had been given a dream – as a young man (17 years old) – that he would have a life of significance. It took a long time for that to come to pass. While he was waiting he was put into a pit by his brothers; then falsely accused and put in prison. He remained faithful and rose to become 2nd in command to Pharaoh, the king of Egypt. Joseph believed in the unbreakable purpose, power, promises and peace of God. We have to be people of faith. He knew this in both the pit and in the palace.*"

Remember, God Himself told us that "*my ways are not your ways, and my thoughts are not your thoughts.*" That also means that God's timings are not our timings, nor is His way of outworking our purpose going to be the way we might plan it; and God is never late!

Perhaps you are even going through a challenging, extended period of trials and testing. If you feel like you are in a refining process, then you can rejoice! That means that God has been watching how you respond to situations and that He knows you and can rely on you. Once you come out the other side, then He will be able to use you in a significant way.

If you believe that God has predestined your life and that He knows the end from the beginning, then you have to trust that in ALL things He knows what's best for you – and that includes where you are planted at this time and your future steps.

Remember, your life and your purpose on this planet are not just about you. God knows precisely how your steps will interweave with the steps of others and how important it is that you are right where you are, right now.

"*Ask, and it will be given to you; seek and you will find; knock, and the door will be opened to you.*" (Matthew 7:7, NIV). Ask God for help in finding peace in the midst of the unknown. Ask Him for clarity. Ask Him for wisdom to know the best way forward, and He will tell you as

He said He would. The Bible is full of special promises, like this one. When we are walking in what seems like a murky haze, it's important to be able to plant our feet on the rock of His Word, and hold fast to what we know to be true amid all the unknowns.

MOSES

OK, so you believe that you have been blessed with gifts, talents, a calling and a God-given, predestined purpose. All you are waiting on now is your assignment, and it seems like you have been waiting forever. It's in times like these that it's worthwhile remembering God's friend, Moses.

Remember that for the first 40 years of Moses' life he lived in a palace. He knew he had a calling on his life, but didn't know how it would outwork. Thinking he could help his people when he saw an act of injustice, Moses murdered an Egyptian man. He tried to rush God's timing for his life.

It was another 40 years before God finally gave Moses the green light to begin his assignment to lead the Israelites out of Egypt and into the Promised Land. Wow, that's 40 long years of waiting, and I can imagine how frustrated and impatient Moses could have been during that time.

Knowing that God has predestined you for a specific purpose, does that mean you will come out of the womb ready to change the world? As far as I am aware, only Jesus had that honour, and even Jesus lived for 30 years on this earth, preparing Himself for God's ultimate assignment for His life. That meant Jesus was ready when God said 'go'.

Waiting is hard – for everybody. Just know that if God has you waiting (even if it's 40 years, like Moses), it's for a good reason – either for your benefit or for His timing.

WINTER

We often talk about having 'seasons' in our life. This concept is reflected in the well-known passage in Ecclesiastes 3:1–8 (NIV), and was made popular by The Byrds with their 1965 song '*Turn! Turn! Turn!*'.

> *"There is a time for everything,*
> *and a season for every activity under the heavens:*
> *a time to be born and a time to die,*
> *a time to plant and a time to uproot,*
> *a time to kill and a time to heal,*
> *a time to tear down and a time to build,*
> *a time to weep and a time to laugh,*
> *a time to mourn and a time to dance,*
> *a time to scatter stones and a time to gather them,*
> *a time to embrace and a time to refrain from embracing,*
> *a time to search and a time to give up,*
> *a time to keep and a time to throw away,*
> *a time to tear and a time to mend,*
> *a time to be silent and a time to speak,*
> *a time to love and a time to hate,*
> *a time for war and a time for peace."*

In the times when you feel like you are going nowhere fast, it can also seem like you are languishing in a 'winter' season of life – cold, barren, perhaps even hopeless. If we understand, from Scripture, that there is a time for everything – even winter – we should dig further to see what God intended when he gave us the winter season. It is also interesting to note that God apportioned winter (depending on the country you live in) to approximately three months of every single year.

CHILL TIME

Some of our favourite garden plants benefit significantly from the cold months when they can store up energy for new growth. For example, cold temperatures stimulate garlic to sprout and develop a bulb, and many fruit trees (such as apple and cherry) have what they call a 'chill time' requirement. Chill time begins as soon as the leaves fall off of the tree and extends to the first bloom. Cherry trees require between 600 and 700 hours of chill time to produce ample, healthy blossoms.

Instead of seeing a 'winter' season as a negative thing, why not try to reframe your perspective? God doesn't ever intend for you to be 'stuck', like gumboots in the mud – that's not His way. Assuming that there are no barriers in your life that you need to deal with, then there will always be a reason for the season. Perhaps God is nurturing you in a period of 'chill time' to rest and reset so that he can ensure you will be ready to generate the most magnificent blooms when springtime comes, and the most delicious fruit in summer.

Patience is one of the nine spiritual 'fruits' talked about in Galatians 5:13–26. Having patience is a sign that you trust God and are willing to wait on His timing and plan for every area of your life.

PESKY PESTS

Winter weather helps to reduce pest populations, especially bugs – the deeper the freeze, the deeper the impact. For example, tiger mosquito eggs will perish below -10°C and a good deep-freeze will affect garden moths as well.

Do you have any pesky pests that you need to deal with in your life (such as sin, mindsets, unhealthy relationships)? It's easy to ignore these pests in summer when times are good, and you're in a season of high productivity. Winter months offer an excellent opportunity for quietness and reflection, when you may be more keenly aware of which pests need dealing with. Now is the time to deep-freeze them off your life.

SNOW REPLENISHES WATERWAYS

Water is an essential natural resource, and many of us know what it's like to live through drought conditions and to be without water. For countries that experience snowfall, they also receive a blessing when the snow melts to replenish tributaries, aquifers, lakes, ponds and streams.

As God Himself said in Isaiah 55:10–11 (NIV): *"As the rain and the snow come down from heaven, and do not return to it without watering the earth and making it bud and flourish, so that it yields seed for the sower and bread for the eater, so is my word that goes out from my mouth: It will not return to me empty, but will accomplish what I desire and achieve the purpose for which I sent it."*

In the winter times, let the rain of God's Word wash over you and replenish your soul, and hold fast to God's promise that His Word will not return empty over your life.

SPRING IS JUST AROUND THE CORNER

As Ecclesiastes reminds us, *"there is a time for everything, and a season for every activity under the heavens."* For every winter, there is also a spring, summer and autumn. If our lives were always lived in a season of summer and contentment, we would likely fall into a sense of complacency. And if we never had winter, how could we ever fully appreciate summer and the warmth that it brings to our lives?

Most of all, don't forget hope. Spring brings a sense of hope, which would be meaningless if it were not for winter: *"…those who hope in the LORD will renew their strength. They will soar on wings like eagles; they will run and not grow weary, they will walk and not be faint."* (Isaiah 40:31, NIV)

If you are experiencing a time of winter and the feeling of hopelessness that it can bring, then warm yourself with this verse. If your hope is in God, and you know that spring is just around the corner, then you also have the surety that God's purposes and plans for your life will work out just as they are meant to do – in God's time, and His appointed season.

THE PARENTING PAUSE BUTTON

I was having a chat about 'purpose' with a friend, who we will call Anna. Anna is the mother to a lively family of four young girls. She mentioned how she and her husband had dreamed (pre-children) of working full-time in Christian ministry, but that life and family had come along, and those dreams were now in a 'holding pattern' during their season of parenthood.

This conversation made me think about a common misconception that we tend to have about purpose – that being a parent is like an adjunct to God's purpose for your life.

If you agree with the notion that God knew exactly when and where you would be born, and who your parents were to be, then it also stands to reason that God knew exactly when and where your children were to be born, and who their parents were to be – and that's you.

Parenting is no small thing. The Bible says in Proverbs 22:6 (NKJV) *"Train up a child in the way he should go, and when he is old, he will not depart from it."* You have a finite amount of time in which to influence your child's life before they head into the world to make their way, and that influence could be a crucial element of how God's purpose will play out in THEIR lives. God never meant your purpose to be all about you – purpose has a generational impact. It's about legacy and influencing others (whether you have children or not).

Parenting is not a reason to press the pause button on living out your purpose, and then to hit the play button as soon as your children leave home. If God has blessed you to be the custodian of a child or children, then being a parent (and all that entails in both effort and time) IS PART OF your purpose.

If you think that each child will be under your care for at least 18 years, then those precious parenting years have to come out of the time you have been allocated on this earth. If the average lifespan is around 80 years, then having a family would take a considerable chunk of your years away if you thought you had to put God's purpose for your life on hold for all that time.

If you have children, then being a parent opens up connections and a world of influence that is unique to you – antenatal groups, pre-schools, schools, Sunday school, coffee groups, support groups, PTAs, school boards, etc.

Living out your purpose happens every single breath of every single minute that God has given you. Ask Him for clarity as to how your purpose will outwork during your busy, child-focused years, and you may be pleasantly surprised by what doors open to you!

TIME

One positive thing that came out of the COVID-19 epidemic of 2020 was that it gave many people around the world an unexpected gift of time.

One could say that we were all thrown into a communal 'holding pattern' that lasted six months or longer. During that time, country borders shut down, businesses closed, families were confined to their homes, and many people were left wondering where to go next (especially those who lost their job in the process).

It was interesting to observe how various friends, family and acquaintances chose to use the time that was given to them. Some people picked up a new hobby; started businesses; encouraged others; found ways to up-skill; took online training courses; read books; or rallied others toward a cause. Some people chose to focus on binge-watching TV. Some sank slowly into depression and despair.

Holding patterns in your life will test your resolve, attitudes, focus and the condition of your heart. Time is a precious and finite commodity, and you are a steward over the time that God has given to you (in all seasons of your life). If He has deliberately placed you in a time of waiting, then He expects you to use that time wisely, so that when He hands you your next assignment, you will be ready to rock.

When you are pushing
on closed doors

WHEN ONE DOOR CLOSES...

I've always been an artistically-inclined person. Right from my youngest Picasso-esque attempts, I have loved participating in all types of art and crafts.

However, as much as I tried (and, believe, me I did try), I was only ever an 'average' artist. I could never find a style that would set me apart from my peers or a niche that would allow me to outwork my skills for money or ministry.

In my 30s I embarked on an art project which I titled '*Canvassing My Friends*'. The project was designed with two objectives in mind: the first was to conquer a long-held fear of failure and a fear of what other people thought about me. The second objective was to see if I could become good at painting. It was now or never!

Facebook was de rigueur at the time, so I planned to work my way through my list of Facebook friends, selecting one person at a time to use as inspiration for one painting. Once finished, I would post a photograph of the painting to my Facebook feed (thus keeping me publicly accountable to the project, and open to critique), and then give the painting to the person who was the source of the inspiration.

After completing 14 paintings, I stopped. I reached an understanding (with myself) that although I loved art, the timing was wrong, and I felt like I was heaving a boulder up a hill, feeling little joy along the way.

The upsides were that I was able to bless 14 people with highly-symbolic and encouraging paintings and I was able to conquer my fears. It was thanks to that project that I have dared to send my writing out into the world – something I now know is part of my purpose.

20 years on and I have returned to artistic endeavours, and have found my niche in creating fibre art with wool and silk. It is now the right season, and – as a result – the time I am investing in my artwork is bearing fruit, which is a great sign of rightness.

God has put talents and interests in you for a reason, so you need to explore the things you love to do to help uncover your purpose. In saying that, you also need to know when to stop (if required) and reset your time and attention to the path and purpose that God has planned for you. Ask God to give you wisdom and clarity when you need it.

Outworking your purpose should have a measure of 'effortlessness' to it. The time when elements of your life come together, and it all seems to make perfect sense, will be your 'a-ha' moment. You know it's God when things 'click'.

If you find you are repeatedly pushing on a door that won't open, you need to ask God why that is. He will respond in one of three ways:

- "*Yes.*"
- "*No, there's something better out there for you*"; or
- "*Not right now.*"

Isn't it a blessing to know that, whichever way you look at it, any of those three options are pretty good? When I thought that God was saying "no" to my art dreams (in my 30s), instead of feeling grief or disappointment, I felt peaceful about it. In a way, it was a relief to know that I didn't have to strive anymore, and I had the assurance that something better would be out there for me where I could still use my creativity – which appeared a short time later in the form of writing.

Writing comes easy for me, but I have also invested a lot of time to develop and refine this ability; and – for my efforts – I've seen fantastic results. In other words, work is still required, but if that effort comes with suffering and pushing vainly on closed doors, then you need to question if it's right for you. If you are struggling and striving, it's a sign that you may not be living within your purpose.

Do you think that God answered every prayer that Jesus prayed, exactly as Jesus would have wished it? In Matthew 26:36–39 (NIV) we read: "*Then Jesus went with his disciples to a place called Gethsemane, and he said to them, "Sit here while I go over there and pray." He took Peter and the two sons of Zebedee along with him, and he began to be sorrowful and troubled. Then he said to them, "My soul is overwhelmed with sorrow to the point of death. Stay here and keep watch with me. Going a little farther, he fell with his face to the ground and prayed, "My Father, if it is possible, may this cup be taken from me. Yet not as I will, but as you will."*

It turned out that God did not answer Jesus' prayer with a "yes", because He was taken away, convicted and crucified. But, we discover that God wasn't saying "no" either; He was saying "I have a better plan for you and for all of mankind. Trust me that I know what's best and I will be with you, no matter what."

FORCING GOD'S HAND

Have you ever heard the saying "don't create an Ishmael while you wait for your Isaac"? That comes from a passage that we read in the Bible about Abraham and his wife Sarah in Genesis 15–21.

Abraham (originally known as Abram) and Sarah (originally known as Sarai) were advanced in years, and they had no children. It seemed as though the promise that God had made to Abraham when he was 75 years old (that he would be the father of many nations) was not going to be kept. You can imagine what Abraham must have been thinking: "Did God really say my descendants would outnumber the stars in the sky?"; "Did I hear God correctly?" Instead of being patient and waiting for God's promise to come to pass, Abraham and Sarah decided to 'help God out'.

Sarah took her Egyptian slave, Hagar, and gave her to Abraham to be his wife (as was an accepted custom in those days). Abraham slept with Hagar, and she gave birth to a baby boy whom they named Ishmael. Abraham was 86 years old when he was born.

25 years after making his promise to Abraham, God fulfilled it when Sarah gave birth to their son, Isaac. She was 90 years old, and Abraham was 100 years old.

While there was great rejoicing in God's faithfulness and provision, what they didn't realise is that by being impatient and forcing God's hand, they had opened up a can of worms by producing Ishmael (when they should have waited for Isaac, whom God had told them would come).

Several remarkable prophecies were made and fulfilled regarding Ishmael and his descendants. It was foretold that Ishmael would be: "*…a wild donkey of a man; his hand will be against everyone and everyone's hand against him, and he will live in hostility toward all his brothers.*" (Genesis 16:12, NIV). Later, God said of Ishmael, "*I will surely bless him; I will make him fruitful and will greatly increase his numbers. He will be the father of twelve rulers, and I will make him into a great nation.*" (Genesis 17:20, NIV).

It turned out that Isaac became the father of the 12 Tribes of Israel, of whom all modern-day Jews are descended. Ishmael was the father of our modern-day Arab and Islamic territories. The decision of Abraham and Sarah to push vainly on closed doors and take matters into their own hands has impacted right down to the international political climate that we know today.

Before we judge Abraham and Sarah's actions too harshly, know that it can be just the same way with us. It is more than likely that at some point in our lives we will experience a frustrating or barren situation. Perhaps you, too, have received a prophetic word that God will do something in your life, but you have not yet seen it come to pass.

You can try to manipulate and manoeuvre and take matters into your own hands to come up with a solution, or you can wait for God to move. Whatever you do, remember the story of Isaac and Ishmael!

"If any of you lacks wisdom, you should ask God, who gives generously to all without finding fault, and it will be given to you. But when you ask, you must believe and not doubt, because the one who doubts is like a wave of the sea, blown and tossed by the wind." (James 1:5–6, NIV)

HOPE AND PATIENCE

"But hope that is seen is no hope at all. Who hopes for what they already have? But if we hope for what we do not yet have, we wait for it patiently." (Romans 8:24–25, NIV)

There will be many things that we will hope for in life and many things for which we will need to wait. Some things (such as Abraham and Sarah waiting for their promise from God to be fulfilled) could take years, or decades to come to pass. How will you respond when you have to hope for things that are – as yet – unseen?

Do you consider yourself to be a patient person? Our daily lives require us to exercise patience, whether the things we face are small or big. Receiving a reprimand; dealing with a difficult co-worker; experiencing conflict with a friend or loved one; getting sick, or waiting on God are all situations that require us to be patient, and it is often easier said than done. So, how can we be patient when we find ourselves in challenging circumstances?

The Bible says *"be joyful in hope, patient in affliction, faithful in prayer."* (Romans 12:12, NIV). In life, we will face many trials. However, as Believers, we can find hope in knowing that we have a loving God who is in control of our lives. When we put our trust in His perfect plan rather than our own, we do not need to feel anxious, worried or impatient.

We do not have to struggle to find patience within ourselves. Instead, when we call upon God, He can give us the strength to be patient. While we may not understand the waiting period we are in, we can rest in the fact that God knows the big picture, while we know just a sliver of detail at that moment.

If you are in the midst of a waiting season, remember that God's plan is bigger than anything you could imagine, and – as His child – He will not withhold good things from you. When you are *"joyful in hope, patient in affliction and faithful in prayer"*, He promises to make a way for you through the desert.

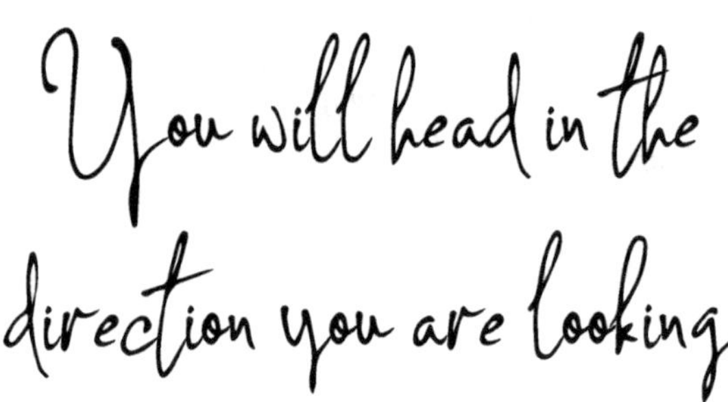

"Let your eyes look straight ahead; fix your gaze directly before you. Give careful thought to the paths for your feet and be steadfast in all your ways. Do not turn to the right or the left; keep your foot from evil." (**Proverbs 4:25–27. NIV**)

For many years, during my 20s, I belonged to a local water-ski club. Before you get too excited (on my behalf), it was my first husband who skied at a national level, not me. While I could master a single ski, I struggled to navigate the slalom course, and so I was never competitive. But, what I did do was spend a LOT of time sitting in the tow boat watching skiers of all levels.

Slalom skiing involves a multi-buoy course that the skier must go around to complete the 'pass'. There are gates (of two buoys) at the beginning and end of the course that the skier must enter and exit, plus there are six 'turn buoys' that the skier must navigate around in a zigzag pattern.

The basic idea of slalom is to make a clean turn around each buoy, get your ski pointed in the right direction, cross the (often unpredictable) boat wake, and get to the next turn buoy – then repeat the process. The key to success is knowing that you will head in the direction that your eyes are looking.

If you snap around the turn buoy, then fix your eyes squarely on the next turn buoy, not only your head, but your shoulders, torso, and ski will automatically follow your eyes. Nine times out of ten, the reason a person fails to reach a turn buoy is that they look up, down or around when they come out of the turn. By that point, they have missed their opportunity, and their pass is over.

As it is in slalom water-skiing, so is it in our own lives and our walk with God – we will head in the direction that our eyes are looking.

The Apostle Paul said we should be *"looking unto Jesus, the author and finisher of our faith."* (Hebrews 12:2, NKJV); and Jesus tells us in John 8:12 (NKJV), *"I am the light of the world. He who follows Me shall not walk in darkness, but have the light of life."* So it is Jesus who is the One on whom we must focus and who we should follow. If we turn our eyes to Jesus, then the rest of our body, mind and spirit will follow suit.

This understanding is critical when you are trying to outwork your God-given purpose. If your eyes are distracted by things that are not God-focused or purpose-focused, then you could start to veer off your path. At the very least, you could waste your time; at the worst, it could result in your relationship and walk with God going awry.

Remember that you tend to get more of what you focus on, so be careful where you invest your time, energy, emotions and thoughts, as what consumes your mind will inevitably control your life (for good or for bad). Keep your relationship with God as your number one focus – if you take care of that, then God will take care of everything else!

Barriers to fulfilling your purpose

Some of the worst barriers you will ever have to face in your life are the ones you create yourself. Life will throw enough challenges your way without you willingly adding to them. Willingly? Yes, indeed, all of the eight barriers that we will talk about in this section are ones that you can either choose to build or choose to turn away from, so let's look at how you can break all these self-made barriers down and get on with living your life in God's purpose!

1 Sin.
2 Unwillingness.
3 Perfectionism.
4 Negative self-talk.
5 Fear.
6 Unbelief.
7 Doubt.
8 Distraction.

1 SIN

The Christian definition of sin means to purposely disobey the rules of God (*"Everyone who sins breaks the law; in fact, sin is lawlessness."* 1 John 3:4, NIV).

The Bible says, "*The wrath of God is being revealed from heaven against all the godlessness and wickedness of people, who suppress the truth by their wickedness, since what may be known about God is plain to them, because God has made it plain to them. For since the creation of the world God's invisible qualities – his eternal power and divine nature – have been clearly seen, being understood from what has been made, so that people are without excuse.*" (Romans 1:18-20, NIV). God commands us to follow moral law and has given every human being a conscience for intuitively knowing right from wrong.

The Christian view is that sin has been with mankind since Adam and Eve's disobedience in the Garden of Eden. Their 'original sin' was to eat fruit from the tree of the knowledge of good and evil that God had told them explicitly not to eat.

From that point in history onwards, we come across hundreds of sins mentioned in the Bible. To help us remember some of the most impacting sins, God condensed them into the Ten Commandments, given to Moses by God in Exodus 20:3–17 (NIV). These laws of "*thou shalt not*" are meant for our protection and guidance. God, our loving Father, wants to give us wisdom and keep us from choices that He knows will harm us.

THE TEN COMMANDMENTS

1 You shall have no other gods before me.
2 You shall not make for yourself an image in the form of anything in heaven above, or on the earth beneath, or in the waters below.
3 You shall not misuse the name of the Lord your God.
4 Remember the Sabbath day by keeping it holy.
5 Honour your father and your mother.
6 You shall not murder.
7 You shall not commit adultery.
8 You shall not steal.
9 You shall not give false testimony against your neighbour.
10 You shall not covet (desire wrongfully).

It is easy to feel burdened by the weight of sin. Sin is a heavy load to place on your spirit, your thoughts and your health.

In Isaiah 59:2 (NIV) it says that "…*your iniquities* [sins] *have separated you from your God; your sins have hidden His face from you so that He will not hear.*" Sin is sin, no matter its perceived size or consequences, and the Bible tells us that all sin – ANY type of sin – separates us from our loving Father God.

The good news is that Jesus Christ – through His death on the cross, and His resurrection – provided the only way for us to cancel out our sins and give us a new, clean, hope-filled future. He took all our sins on his shoulders and paid the price that we would have otherwise paid. Jesus Christ died for you so that you might experience true love, life, hope, and joy.

"*Therefore, if anyone is in Christ, he is a new creation; old things have passed away; behold, all things have become new. Now all things are of God, who has reconciled us to Himself through Jesus Christ, and has given us the ministry of reconciliation, that is, that God was in Christ reconciling the world to Himself, not imputing their trespasses* [sins] *to them, and has committed to us the word of reconciliation.*" (2 Corinthians 5:17–19, NKJV)

Jesus Christ came to earth to "*seek and to save the lost*" (Luke 19:10, NIV), giving each of us a way to be cleansed of our sins, and offering us the chance to spend eternity with Him in heaven. All we have to do is take Him up on the offer.

SIN IN YOUR PAST

In 1993 the Christian singer, Carman, released his '*Revival in the Land*' album. On a track of the same name, he wrote this imagined conversation between Satan and his chief demon lieutenant:

Demon: *The bad news is the subject of their prayers that threatens our survival. What they're praying for is causing haemorrhaging in the realms of darkness.*

Satan: *And the bad news is?*

Demon: *Sir, they're praying for revival!*
Satan: *I hate revival, it just erupts, it's hardly controllable. At the Azusa street outpouring, things got rough.*
Demon: *Yes sir, and when the charismatic movement hit, sir, we were jumping out of windows with all that "untie my bow tie who stole-a my Honda" stuff.*
Satan: *Then I'll come in like a flood.*
Demon: *But they'll say the Spirit of the Lord will lift up a standard against you.*
Satan: *OOOOHH.*
Demon: *It's written in the Word.*
Satan: *I'll form weapons against them.*
Demon: *Sir, no weapon formed against them shall prosper. That's in the Bible, too.*
Satan: *Yes, I've heard. I'll hit them with every filthy, lusty thought you could imagine.*
Demon: *But it's written, "resist the devil and he must flee."*
Satan: *Obviously, the enemy is taking the battle more seriously than we are.*
Demon: *And that's very dangerous, sir, especially for me.*
Satan: *It's time to launch my final, most vicious attack. I'll remind the saints of their past – how they were liars, cheaters, manipulators and moochers.*
Demon: *But sir, you know what will happen if you remind the saints of their past?*
Satan: *And what is that?*
Demon: *Sir, they'll just remind you of your future.*

Every single one of us has a 'past' – a life before we started a relationship with God through Jesus Christ. For you, this past life may have been filled with wrongdoing and things of which you may be highly-ashamed. You may even think that your past sins are worse, or more 'unforgivable' than other people's.

If you allow Satan to speak into your life, he will try to convince you to remain in the past. However, by doing this, you are not only blocking God from working in your life, but you are also – in effect – denying what Jesus Christ did for you on the cross. So, the next time that Satan tries to throw your past in your face (and it's guaranteed that he will try) remember who you are in Christ.

Yes, you may have done some regrettable things. Yes, you may be living the consequences of your actions. However, God looks at your heart, and if He says that your heart is clean, it's clean. If He says that you are a new creation, believe it. You can't change your past, but Jesus Christ has wiped that slate clean so that you can focus on your future. That's a wonderful gift to be celebrated!

SIN IN YOUR PRESENT

The sin-debt that Jesus paid for us on the cross dealt with the sins of our past, bridged the gap between God and us, and gave us hope for an eternal future with Him. Does that then mean that we stop sinning as Christians? Unfortunately, no.

God created us with a free will to choose. We can choose life from death, right from wrong, black from white – and we will have to make those choices daily for the rest of our time here on earth, which means there will be a lot of opportunities to let sinful thoughts and actions creep in.

The power that sin can have over us, and the way it affects our relationship with God, makes it one of the primary barriers to us living within the purpose that God has predestined, and stops us living an abundant life.

Are you making sinful choices? Is your conscience being pricked? Do you feel an absence of God's blessing on your life or a sense of aimlessness? Are you doing, saying or thinking ungodly things? God will challenge you (directly or through others), but ultimately you need to decide which way you will go and take action.

An interesting fact is that in both Hebrew and Greek, the word 'sin' means 'to miss the mark', and in both languages, it is also an archery term. Have you missed the mark in your walk with God? If so, here is an outline, prepared by Dr Henry W. Wright, on how to get yourself back into alignment:

8 Rs to Freedom

1 **Recognise**. Recognise the issue in your life that is not from God, or the sin that you participated in.
2 **Responsibility**. Take personal responsibility (for what you recognise) with God our Father.
3 **Repent**. Repent (show regret or remorse) to God for participating in what you recognised.
4 **Renounce**. Make what you recognised your enemy and renounce it (make a 180° turn away from your sin).
5 **Remove**. Remove the sin from your life. Cast it out once and for all.
6 **Resist**. Draw near to God and resist the sin coming back to you. Refuse to get involved with it ever again.
7 **Rejoice**. Give thanks to God for setting you free.
8 **Restore**. Help to restore others held captive by sin.

2 UNWILLINGNESS

In the Book of Genesis, we read about how Abraham wanted to secure a wife for his son (Isaac) before he died. So Abraham commissioned his most trusted servant to find a suitable bride from the land of his birth, saying to him, *"See to it that you do not take my son back there. The Lord, the God of heaven, who took me from my father's house and from the land of my kindred, and who spoke to me and swore to me, 'To your offspring, I will give this land,' He will send his angel before you, and you shall take a wife for my son from there. But if the woman is not willing to follow you, then you will be free from this oath of mine."* (Genesis 24:6–8, ESV)

The servant, through God's help, identified Rebekah as being the woman who God intended as Isaac's bride, but – ultimately – the decision on the union was up to Rebekah.

We then read what I believe to be one of the most powerful statements in all of scripture: *"But Isaac's servant said to them, "Do not delay me, since the Lord has prospered my way. Send me away that I may go to my master." They said, "Let us call the young woman and ask her." And they called Rebekah and said to her, "Will you go with this man?" She said, "**I will go.**""* (Genesis 24: 56–58, ESV, emphasis added)

This passage spoke to me at a time when I was unwilling to do something. It was 2005, and we were living in Kerikeri in the beautiful Bay of Islands, New Zealand.

Simon had attended a local church-hosted meeting where the guest speaker was the then-head of Bridges for Peace, a long-standing American Christian organisation headquartered in Jerusalem, Israel.

A while after the event, Simon asked me if I would consider moving to Israel to work with Bridges for Peace. My immediate and vehement reaction was *"no way"*. We continued this predictable dialogue over some time, with Simon asking if I'd be open to considering the move, and me always saying *"no"*. When asked *"why"*, my reply would be that I didn't want to uproot my life which I quite enjoyed at the time (my beautiful home, my successful business, my friends, my church, me, me, me…).

Eventually, my self-focused walls started to break down. I decided to make a deal with God in a similar way that Gideon did in Judges 6:36–40. The expression 'to put out a fleece' comes from the passage in scripture where Gideon requests God's guarantee of victory through two tests. In the first test, Gideon puts a fleece garment on the ground and asks God to miraculously cause dew to only collect on the garment, not on the rest of the ground. In the second test, Gideon reverses his request and asks for the fleece to be dry and the ground to be covered with dew.

More out of desperation than thinking I was somehow better than Gideon, I asked God for three, clear signs that we were to move to

Israel, and He didn't disappoint (he gave me three-and-a-half!). The point being is that God is faithful and extremely patient. I not only questioned God's call on our life, I asked Him to prove that it was really Him making the request and not just us moving for the sake of a whim or a good idea.

God did what I can only describe as a work in my heart that led to a 180° change in attitude. I went from an unwilling person to one who said "I will go", thereby making a heart-shift into a place of obedience to follow God's call, assignment and purpose.

Simon and I moved to Jerusalem in April 2006, aligned with Bridges for Peace. We gave away or sold almost everything that we had, bought a one-way ticket for ourselves and our two dogs, and moved to the other side of the world. At that point, there was no long-term plan, only a willingness to do what God required of us with open and obedient hearts.

God will never force you to do anything you do not wish to do. He prefers to work with someone willing and someone who will step outside their comfort zone. He will create the opportunities and extend the invitation, but you still have to accept His calling or assignment or request.

Have you ever heard of the phrase 'to dig one's heels (or toes) in'? It means to stubbornly resist or refuse to do something. Do you have any unwillingness in your heart that needs to be dealt with? If so, you may find this to be the starting point for moving forward in the purpose that God has for your life. Believe me; it's worth it to find out!

3 PERFECTIONISM

In 1996 the late British singer, George Michael, performed on MTV Unplugged – a live, televised event which left the artist no margin for error. I remember watching a documentary about George Michael which focused on this performance in particular, covering both the preparation and the event. In the documentary, he talked about how his desire for perfectionism could – at times – manifest like a debilitating disease, to the point where he felt like he couldn't sing at all.

Even if you don't like his music, it's undeniable that George Michael had one of the strongest, most precise and effortless voices of his time. It's difficult to believe that someone with his degree of talent could become paralysed by perfectionism.

Let's look at a few definitions:

- **Perfect.** Entirely without any flaws, defects, or shortcomings. Accurate, exact, or correct in every detail.
- **Perfection**. The state or quality of being or becoming perfect.
- **Perfectionism**. A personal standard, attitude, or philosophy that demands perfection and rejects anything less.
- **Excellent**. Possessing outstanding quality or superior merit; remarkably good.
- **Excellence**. The quality of being outstanding or extremely good. (Dictionary app; oxforddictionaries.com)

Trying to achieve perfection in aspects of your life is an ambitious goal. Indeed, people around you may appreciate it if you were flawless in all of your endeavours, perhaps nodding their heads and saying "*well done*". However, what would be the cost of pursuing perfection, and is that pursuit worth it (or even necessary)?

Human beings are naturally-flawed creatures. We live a continuous cycle of making mistakes, learning from those mistakes, and improving. Rarely could a person reach perfection in any one thing (let alone a range of things) and yet some people drive themselves relentlessly toward this goal. As in the case of George Michael, some people reach a point where they can no longer achieve forward momentum and hit a perfection-shaped wall.

Even if you did manage to achieve a state of perfection, sustaining it would be nigh-on impossible (ask any top sportsperson). This retro-grading is supported by the 'Law of Disorder' which (loosely summarised) says that everything (no matter how perfect it may at one time be) will gradually decline into disorder.

The pursuit of perfection can come at a personal cost to your physical health and mental well-being, and then – subsequently – at a cost to those around you.

Your energy and effort will serve you far better if you strive for 'excellence' rather than 'perfection'. Excellence ('the quality of being outstanding or extremely good') is both realistic and attainable. It is a journey rather than a destination and something that could and should filter through everything you do.

4 NEGATIVE SELF-TALK

There are two different types of negative self-talk: that which goes on silently in your head, and that which you speak out loud (to yourself or others).

TALKING INSIDE YOUR HEAD

I tend to refer to internal monologue as 'theatre'. Do you ever find yourself re-running episodes of your life over and over again? Do you try the scene with different words; different endings; different players? Perhaps you play out scenarios of conversations yet-to-happen. What will I say? What will they say? If I say this, then that will happen, etc.

What part do you play in those 'theatre'-based conversations? I bet that it's not a particularly confident or positive version of yourself. How do I know this? Because playing theatre in your mind is a sign of a person who does not have their assurance or trust firmly in God. It's a sign of worry, anxiety and self-deprecation.

Up until my late 20s, I'm sure I held the best internal theatre shows around. I could replay both past and future scenes from my life in extraordinary detail, and I was a master of the 'if/then' game: "if I say this, and they say this, then this will happen."

I grew to understand that the more I allowed this type of theatre to happen, the more I lived in a fantasy world, and – as a result – was blocking God out of my life. I was trusting in myself to work out situations, rather than giving them over to Him to help me.

How did I stop? Firstly, I had to recognise what I was doing and that it was an unhealthy practice. Secondly, I consciously and willingly let the performances go and refused to participate. Whenever I caught myself opening the theatre curtains, I would instead pray to God about the situation. Eventually, this old habit died away, and I formed a new (prayerful) habit. It was a case of letting go of the past and dealing with things such as unforgiveness and hurt. I also had to learn to trust God to help me navigate an unknown future, with a peaceful heart and belief that He would be walking with me every step of the way.

Internal monologues and theatre shows are dangerous. They will seek to trap you in your past and give you a warped view of your future – both of which will greatly reduce your effectiveness to move boldly in God's plans for your life. Remember, *"Cast all your anxiety on Him because He cares for you."* (1 Peter 5:7, NIV)

TALKING OUT LOUD

This is the type of self-talk we can all identify with, and one that is incredibly dangerous. In our section on 'Influence', we talked about how *"death and life are in the power of the tongue."* (Proverbs 18:21, NKJV), and I'll give you a first-hand example of just how powerful the spoken word can be.

In the late-90s I attended a mid-sized Presbyterian church in the south of Auckland and was part of a thriving 20-somethings youth group.

We wanted to bless the elderly in our community and decided on a visit to the geriatric ward at Middlemore Hospital. We were to sing Christian songs to the patients there, which would happen on a Sunday directly after church.

The night before, we gathered together to do a final practice and work out the logistics for the day. As I headed off to my car, someone called out *"see you tomorrow"*. I remember what I replied, word-for-word, which was *"I'll be there. The only thing that can keep me away is laryngitis!"*

The next morning I went to church, feeling healthy as a horse. Part way through the service I started to cough – just sporadically and gently at first, then my breathing became laboured, and I knew something was wrong.

The local Accident & Emergency clinic was just around the corner, so that was my first port of call. However, they soon had me in an ambulance, on a breathing machine, heading to Middlemore Hospital.

I ended up staying two days in the same hospital where our group sang to the patients; in the ward right next to the geriatric ward; with a diagnosis of viral laryngitis.

Beware of the words that come out of your mouth! Death could have been in the power of my tongue that day, and the incident was no mere coincidence. The hospital trip was of my choosing, based on the words that I had declared over myself. I had no-one to blame but me.

The apostle James talked a lot about taming the tongue in James 3:5–12 (NIV):

"Consider what a great forest is set on fire by a small spark. The tongue also is a fire, a world of evil among the parts of the body. It corrupts the whole body, sets the whole course of one's life on fire, and is itself set on fire by hell.

"All kinds of animals, birds, reptiles and sea creatures are being tamed and have been tamed by mankind, but no human being can tame the tongue. It is a restless evil, full of deadly poison.

"With the tongue we praise our Lord and Father, and with it we curse human beings, who have been made in God's likeness. Out of the same mouth come praise and cursing. My brothers and sisters, this should not be. Can both fresh water and salt water flow from the same spring? My brothers and sisters, can a fig tree bear olives, or a grapevine bear figs? Neither can a salt spring produce fresh water."

What words are you declaring over your life (either inside your head or out loud)? Do you use any of the following words (or similar) about yourself: I'm stupid/silly/dumb/clumsy/accident-prone/unlovable; I'm not worth it; there's no use; I'm such a disappointment; I can't do it; I'll never follow through; people won't like me; others are better than I am; I am not enough; I must be perfect; I can never do anything right; my opinion doesn't matter; I'll never be any different. Does any of this sound familiar? Perhaps you think you are 'joking' when you say these words, and that you don't mean them. Really? My mother used to say "never a truer word was said in jest", and I agree.

Have you heard of the term 'self-fulfilling prophecy'? This is a sociological term rather than a biblical one, and it's used to describe a prediction that causes itself to become true. In this instance, it means if you think a particular way about yourself, and you declare that belief over your life with your words, it's highly likely it will come to pass, whether the notion is based in fact or not.

If you are making negative declarations over your life (or over other people) – big words, small words, joking words, serious words – please, stop now. As in our 'theatre' example, the first way to put an end to negative self-talk is to learn to notice when you are self-critical. For example, take note of when you say things to yourself that you would never say to a good friend or a child.

Remember that thoughts and feelings are not always grounded in reality. Thinking negative things about yourself may feel like astute observations, but your thoughts can easily be skewed and influenced by your moods, biases and events.

Learn to recognise the voice of your Father God. His is the voice of love, peace, goodness, and faithfulness. Once we recognise His voice, we can more easily determine if another voice is false or a counterfeit. The best way to discern His voice is to read the Bible (God's word) consistently. That way, you will be able to use God's own words to counteract any negativity either inside your head, words you speak, or words that are being spoken to you.

When you hear yourself saying negative self-talk, write the words down so you can address them in turn. How many of these words are rooted in fear? Don't be surprised if all of them are. Find scriptures that relate to these thoughts and fears and then declare the scriptures as positive affirmations over your life.

For the sake of your mental, spiritual and physical health, your walk with God and the outworking of your purpose, I urge you to replace all negative words with those that encourage life, positivity and fruitfulness.

5 FEAR

Whether you are a born again, Bible-believing Christian or not, life will inevitably present you with challenges and confronting experiences. It's entirely conceivable that you will feel a sense of fear or anxiety in various facets of your life (home, work, hobbies, church, etc.). You'll recognise the sensation: a quickened heartbeat, shortness of breath, racing mind or perhaps a feeling of being smothered by your circumstances.

Fear can be a compelling motivator for some people, but – most often – it's just plain destructive. It will rob you of your joy and steal your strength to fight for your purpose. Fear exists in good times as well as the bad, and it can hit you at any point.

There is a well-known Bible verse that tells us *"for God has not given us a spirit of fear, but of power and of love and of a sound mind."* (2 Timothy 1:7, NIV). Fear is not of God and has no place in the life of a Christian. It is debilitating and will directly prevent you from living out the plans and purposes that God has for you.

Fear is one of Satan's most highly-effective and frequently-used tools. Therefore, he will throw every fear he can, at you, to stop you living an abundant, God-focused life.

Human beings have just two innately-wired (in-built) fears: the fear of loud noises and the fear of falling – both designed to keep us safe. That means ALL other fears are learned fears.

So, what can you do about fear in your life? 1 John 4 gives us the answer:

"This is how we know that we live in Him and He in us: He has given us of His Spirit. And we have seen and testify that the Father has sent His Son to be the Saviour of the world. If anyone acknowledges that Jesus is the Son of God, God lives in them and they in God. And so we know and rely on the love God has for us.

*"God is love. Whoever lives in love lives in God, and God in them. This is how love is made complete among us so that we will have confidence on the day of judgment: In this world, we are like Jesus. **There is no fear in love. But perfect love drives out fear**, because fear has to do with pun-ishment. The one who fears is not made perfect in love."* (1 John 4:13–18, NIV, emphasis added)

From this passage, we know that *"perfect love drives out fear"*, and that *"God is love"*. Therefore, if you are experiencing fear in your life, you need to name it and bring the fear to the light; renounce it; release it, and ask God to fill you with His perfect love.

PROCRASTINATION

We all procrastinate sometimes, despite knowing that it has a neg-ative impact on our productivity. The word 'procrastinate' comes from the Latin roots 'pro' (forward) and 'crastinus' (belonging to tomorrow), which developed into English, meaning 'deferred until tomorrow'.

So, why do we knowingly put important things off that we know we need to do? Some forms of procrastination stem from laziness, but I believe the chief cause is subconscious fear. Let's take a look at the four fears I believe contribute most to procrastination:

1 **Fear of failure.** This is a massive factor in procrastination because it includes so many related fears: fear you'll do the job badly; fear you didn't prepare enough; fear because you don't know where to start; fear you don't know enough; and so on. Ultimately, you fear you'll mess up the task and look foolish, and maybe you will; but if you let procrastination weigh you down, your self-fulfilling proph-ecy (as we read earlier) will more than likely come to pass, and you

will fail anyway! The best way to move forward is to prepare carefully, do the best you can, and deal with any issues as they emerge.

2   **Fear of success.** This fear is also surprisingly common. You may have heard the saying that 'the best ditch digger's reward is a bigger shovel and more work'. You may think that success in your endeavours will bring you more work and – therefore – more stress and so you would prefer to procrastinate and fail than face the alternative. In John 15:5–8 (NIV) Jesus Christ himself says: "*I am the vine; you are the branches. If you remain in me and I in you, you will bear much fruit; apart from me you can do nothing. If you do not remain in me, you are like a branch that is thrown away and withers; such branches are picked up, thrown into the fire and burned. If you remain in me and my words remain in you, ask whatever you wish, and it will be done for you. This is to my Father's glory, that you bear much fruit, showing yourselves to be my disciples.*" Did you catch the solution? The only way we can do the hard things God gives us to do is in union with him, and that bearing 'much fruit' is the goal and not to be feared!

3   **Fear of the unknown.** When a situation presents that is new to you, or that's unclear, you may feel reluctant to put your shoulder to the wheel and get to work. Fear of the unknown is a common fear to have when (not if) God pushes you outside of your comfort zone. As with any other fear, you first need to give that fear to God so you can deal with it on a spiritual level. Then, practically-speaking, you can also overcome this fear by consulting with someone who has experienced your situation before, and by acquiring knowledge or tools to help you move forward with confidence.

4   **Fear of the task.** This fear arises when you're given something you don't like to do, possibly because it's difficult, unpleasant, you're sick of it, or you feel unqualified for it. So, instead, you do other things first, deferring your lesser-preferred task until tomorrow. At least you're procrastinating somewhat productively, but you're still

procrastinating, and God's work is still not getting done.

There's a saying in popular culture that goes 'feel the fear and do it anyway', and there is merit in that advice. You have a choice: you can let your fears control you, or you can square your shoulders and do the work you need to do. If you procrastinate about the things that God wants you to do, how will your Godly assignments ever get done?

You need to lay aside any fears in your life and give them to God. Tell him your concerns and ask Him to show you what needs to be done and how to do it. God will not let you flounder, but you need to be the one who asks for help.

6 UNBELIEF

If you read a dictionary definition of the word 'unbelief' it will say something like "*the state or quality of not believing; incredulity or scepticism, especially in matters of doctrine or religious faith*".

From a Christian point of view, 'unbelief' means to believe something other than what God has said about a situation. For example, you can believe Jesus was raised from the dead, you can believe He is your Lord, you can believe God the Father created the world and everything in it, but if you don't believe and do what He says, you are operating in unbelief. You can believe in Him, but still not believe what He says. The Bible calls this an 'evil heart' – a 'hardened heart' (Hebrews 3:12), and a heart of unbelief grieves God.

Why is belief so important? Because "*If you can believe, all things are possible*" (Mark 9:23, NKJV). And that's where God wants us to live – in the realm of what is possible through Him, and Him alone. That's what sets Christians apart from a lost and hopeless world.

Are you questioning God? Are you waiting for a work of God in your life today? Have you been spinning your wheels, wanting to move forward in God's purpose for your life, but never quite gaining traction? Maybe you are facing a challenge or assignment so big, and you don't know how you'll overcome it, so you just stay put.

If this sounds like you, then you've probably prayed about your situation over and over again. You may be wondering why haven't things improved, or why hasn't your request been answered? Jesus Christ gives us the answer in Matthew 17:14–21 (NKJV):

"And when they had come to the multitude, a man came to [Jesus], kneeling down to Him and saying, "Lord, have mercy on my son, for he is an epileptic and suffers severely; for he often falls into the fire and often into the water. So I brought him to Your disciples, but they could not cure him."

"Then Jesus answered and said, "O faithless and perverse generation, how long shall I be with you? How long shall I bear with you? Bring him here to Me." And Jesus rebuked the demon, and it came out of him; and the child was cured from that very hour.

"Then the disciples came to Jesus privately and said, "Why could we not cast it out?"

"So Jesus said to them, "Because of your unbelief; for assuredly, I say to you, if you have faith as a mustard seed, you will say to this mountain, 'Move from here to there,' and it will move; and nothing will be impossible for you."

It can be tough to hear, but it is unbelief that is the cause of so much defeat and inaction in the lives of Christians. It's not that we don't want to believe, for the most part; it's that we haven't learned how to overcome the tiniest bit of unbelief that may reside in our hearts. Often, we don't even know it's there until we take a closer look and bring the unbelief to the light.

To help, here are three ways you can dig out the weeds of unbelief:

1 **Know the will and the Word of God.** *"So then faith comes by hearing, and hearing by the word of God."* (Romans 10:17, NKJV). Ignorance is Satan's playground. He knows if he can keep you from knowing all that belongs to you, he has you. A lack of knowledge results in unbelief, and Satan is right there to take advantage, telling you you're useless, sick, depressed and a failure – the direct opposite of what God wants you to hear. But Satan can be over-

ruled by the Word of God, and if you know this, you can object to his claims. If you don't, you'll buy what he is selling and stay right where you are.

2 **Reject fear and worry.** "*For I, the Lord your God, will hold your right hand, saying to you, 'Fear not, I will help you.'*" (Isaiah 41:13, NKJV). The basis of all unbelief is fear. If you don't deal with it (like we talked about previously), it will begin to work on your mind, and you will question the Word of God and the plans He has for your life. Did you know that worry is also a form of unbelief, and that it is impossible to worry and trust God at the same time? Don't let fear have the last word about your situation. Simply negate the fear-based words that you have been saying or thinking. Then, in Jesus' name, declare positive scripture-based truths over your life, such as; "*I believe I am a child of God*"; "*I believe He has a plan for my life*"; "*I believe that my God will supply all my needs*"; etc.

3 **Believe in God's love.** "*And we have known and believed the love that God has for us. God is love, and he who abides in love abides in God, and God in him.*" (1 John 4:16, NKJV). We're not talking about just any love, but THE love. God is love – He doesn't just have love, He IS love! The love of God is a powerful force that has provided you with abundant life, but many Christians don't have faith in His love.

We see an example of unbelief when the disciples were on a ship that was threatened by a great storm. "*Jesus was in the stern, sleeping on a cushion. The disciples woke him and said to him, "Teacher, don't you care if we drown?" He got up, rebuked the wind and said to the waves, "Quiet! Be still!" Then the wind died down, and it was completely calm. He said to his disciples, "Why are you so afraid? Do you still have no faith?*" (Mark 4:38–40, NIV).

Maybe today, you're saying the same thing, "*Jesus, don't You care that*

I'm floundering?" "Don't You care that I'm in a bad situation?" "Don't You care that things aren't going my way?" And that's where we get it wrong. God (who is love) does not put sickness on anyone. He does not put poverty on anyone. Love (who is God) hates sin and its horrible off-spring, which are sickness, disease, weakness, pain and poverty. God does not want to put you in a place of difficulty; He wants to see you walking in fruitfulness!

That's why Mark 11:22 says: "*Have faith in God.*" We know God is love, so what this verse is also saying is have faith in love. Believe the love. Receive the love, and believe the mercy that endures forever. By doing this, you will begin to see a change in your life.

7 DOUBT

To many people, the word 'doubt' is considered to be synonymous and interchangeable with the word 'unbelief'. For the purpose of this book, I'd like to look at doubt in a slightly different way – not doubt about God Himself, but about how He works through us.

Over the past few years, I have written two industry books – one for advertising, and one for marketing. Both books have been awarded in international book awards, at the highest level possible for business-related, non-fiction subject matter. In the eyes of the world, this recognition reflects a strong ability to write well.

Despite these undeniable peer-based affirmations about my gifts and skills, a curious phenomenon happens inside my head regularly. I can read something that I have written, and think "*golly, that's well-worded, or insightful*", and then have to remind myself that it was I who wrote the words. It's as if my head-knowledge says "*yes, you can write well*", but (for whatever reason) I don't fully accept it at the heart-level. It's an odd feeling – not a deliberate attempt at denial, but rather a subconscious disconnection from the truth. It's as if sometimes I am looking at my life in the 3rd-person perspective, like an outsider looking in.

Have you ever experienced something like this before?

When I try to look objectively at this situation, I can only attribute the feeling to doubt (which we know is closely akin to unbelief). That means I tend to doubt my God-given ability, which in turn implies that I diminish God's support and promotion of that ability.

Doubt, repression or denial of your abilities can completely cripple you, and prevent you from moving in God's purpose for your life. Likewise, God may ask you to do something that you do not feel fully-equipped to do, and so you may start to back-pedal, doubting that God will be there to help you along the way.

The opposite of doubt is faith, certainty, conviction, confidence and trust in God (even when you can't yet see evidence of success). You will know you are reaching a breakthrough when you can confidently say *"I can do all this through Him who gives me strength."* (Philippians 4:13, NIV), and truly mean it.

God wants to help you to finish what He has started: *"…being confident of this, that He who began a good work in you will carry it on to completion until the day of Christ Jesus."* (Philippians 1:6, NIV), and that's an encouraging thought!

8 DISTRACTION

Once you are moving in your assignments, Satan will want to pull you away from doing God's work and cause the maximum damage he possibly can. Satan has many tactics, which can include trying to damage your integrity, discredit you, or remove you from your position of influence (all of which you should be on alert for); but perhaps the most subtle and successful tactic that Satan uses is to tempt and distract you. You may not be able to avoid temptation, but you can certainly choose whether or not that temptation will lead to distraction!

How often have you laid aside time to work on a kingdom-focused task only to fill that time with something else that catches your eye — perhaps an interesting series on TV; or a friend invites you out for a meal, or you find a riveting new novel to read? Perhaps the distraction is something even larger that will consume a lot of your time over a longer period, such as joining a new committee or taking up a new hobby. Perhaps the distraction is a temptation that will cause you to turn your eyes away from your path and – instead – walk into sin.

Beware of temptations and distractions (large and small) that can creep in and encroach on your time and attention (and heart), and lead you away from doing what you know is important.

Reframing failure

DEFINITIONS:

- **Mistake.** An act or judgement that is misguided or wrong; something, especially a word, figure, or fact, which is not correct; an inaccuracy; be wrong about.
- **Failure.** Lack of success; an unsuccessful person or thing; the neglect or omission of expected or required action; the action or state of not functioning.

MISTAKES

It's a sad truth that even the most proficient of human beings will make significant mistakes throughout their lives, especially in their younger years. Mistakes can be made due to a lack of experience - when you have not yet built up enough frames of reference in your memory to access when you need to solve a problem or approach a task. At other times mistakes are made due to a lack of focus, lack of attention-to-detail, or lack of care.

The upside about making a mistake is you will learn a valuable lesson as a result. The downside is that there will be a cost to someone: yourself, your family, your employer, or even society. The cost may be a loss of time, money, business, reputation, respect, or trust.

Mistakes, bad choices, and poor judgement calls should be taken very seriously. It is easy to laugh off a mistake, especially when the cost is not coming directly out of your own pocket. You could flippantly think that others around you will absorb the error and that no-one will mind. The reality is that whoever was affected by your mistake just lost something as a result of your action or inaction.

FAILURE

The interesting thing about mistakes is that a mistake (in of itself) is not necessarily a 'failure', and because you make mistakes (or fail) doesn't make you a 'failure' personally.

The word 'failure' has an incredibly strong connotation and stigma attached to it, and we need to be careful about how we pin that word to our lives and to the lives of the people around us.

There is no inherent blame or shame in the word itself (although it is often inferred). The reality is that we all 'fail' to reach expectations on a daily basis in our personal, professional and spiritual lives, but that doesn't mean we are a 'failure', especially not in God's eyes.

Proverbs 24:16 (NIV) says that "…*for though the righteous fall seven times, they rise again, but the wicked stumble when calamity strikes.*" This verse is saying that even those who walk hand-in-hand with God ('the righteous') will fall at times. Thankfully, the verse also says that 'they rise again'. We get a great illustration of this concept when we look at the life of the Apostle Paul.

We read in Romans 15:24, 25, 28 (NIV) that during Paul's fourth missionary journey, God's wish was for Paul to go to Spain. However, Paul desired to go to Jerusalem. He was warned three times by the Holy Spirit not to go (Acts 21:4-9, 10-13), but he disobeyed (Acts 21:14-17).

Once he reached Jerusalem, Paul made another big mistake by taking bad advice from the local church leaders and compromised his doctrine (Acts 21:20-24). One could say that he 'failed' through his disobedience to God and a series of poor decisions.

Because of these mistakes, Paul spent the next four years in prison. That would be enough to keep the average person in despair, but not Paul. Paul acknowledged the error of his ways and used the opportunity that he had to atone for his actions. It was during this time of imprisonment that he rebounded and wrote his letters to the Philippians, Ephesians, Colossians, and Philemon while under house arrest.

Philippians 3:4–8, 12–19 describes Paul's perspective as a spiritually-adult Believer having recovered from his mistakes who continued his spiritual advance. Did Paul 'fail'? Yes. Was he a 'failure'? No.

FAIL FORWARD

"I missed more than 9000 shots in my career. I've lost more than 300 games. 26 times I've been trusted to take the game-winning shot and missed. I've failed over, and over, and over again in my life. And that is why I succeed." (Michael Jordan, Nike commercial)

Anyone doing anything of note will make mistakes, and will 'fail' at times. In your journey with God (undertaking His assignments, moving in your calling and obediently carrying out God's purpose for your life) you will experience times of failure. While that's never a pleasant prospect, it's reality, so when (not if) the time comes, the ideal scenario is that you 'fail forward'.

Making mistakes is one way that everyone develops and learns (unfortunately), and much of your learning will come via trial and error. 'Failing forward' simply means to learn quickly from your mistakes, rather than 'failing backwards' and repeating the same errors over again. John C. Maxwell writes *"The difference between average people and achieving people is their perception and response to failure."* Aim to be the type of person who responds well, is not afraid to fail, is humble when they do, and uses each experience to grow in both character and skill.

Therefore you need to move through the tough times (acknowledging the facts and feelings of the mistake), learn, let go, and never forget what the process has taught you. Every learning experience should be a step forward.

Remember, every single person makes mistakes. Everyone. Failure should never define you – it's what you do when you fail that counts.

A DIVINE STOP SIGN

I've had some wonderful successes in my life, but I have also had to deal with some impressive failures, the most notable being:

- A broken engagement.
- My first marriage ending in divorce.
- Owning a retail business that closed after only nine months.
- Smaller business ideas that never left the ground; and
- Running a not-for-profit that closed after a short time.

If you are not careful, failure in an aspect of your life can create a type of paralysis which stops you moving forward. Any one of my failures could have stunted me to the point where I was too scared to dip my toe in the water again, but I refused to let that happen. Instead, I took on board as many learnings as I could and kept pushing forward. Failure helped me to learn more about myself, more about the world, and more about God.

I also now realise that what I call my 'failures' were also instances where God put a big ol' stop sign in front of my face. My failures were things I shouldn't have been doing. I was moving in the wrong direction, or spending wasted time and resources in a particular area, or even totally missing the mark in my understanding of what God wanted me to do. Also, in all the instances of failure that I can remember, I experienced an almost total lack of God's blessing and provision. The writing had been well and truly on the wall!

Looking back objectively, I can see how God has been able to take my mistakes, missteps and poor judgement calls, and weave them together in what is now the fabric of my life.

Anyone who has attempted any form of needlework will know that the front can look beautiful, while the reverse side hides a jumbled mass of threads and ends. That's how God works – He takes our messy attempts at life and helps us to create a masterpiece.

Remember, you may have failed, but you are not a failure. Never let Satan drop that lie into your spirit, or let him rob you of your vision, dreams and purpose. You are a precious child of God, and He will pick you up, dust you off, and tell you that you are loved – every single time!

'YOU SAY'
LAUREN DAIGLE

I keep fighting voices in my mind that say I'm not enough.
Every single lie that tells me I will never measure up.
Am I more than just the sum of every high and every low?
Remind me once again just who I am, because I need to know.

You say I am loved when I can't feel a thing.
You say I am strong when I think I am weak.
And You say I am held when I am falling short.
And when I don't belong, oh, You say I am Yours.
And I believe, oh, I believe.
What You say of me.
I believe.

The only thing that matters now is everything You think of me.
In You I find my worth, in You I find my identity.

You say I am loved when I can't feel a thing.
You say I am strong when I think I am weak.
And You say I am held when I am falling short.
When I don't belong, oh, You say I am Yours.
And I believe, oh, I believe.
What You say of me.
Oh, I believe.

Taking all I have and now I'm layin' it at Your feet.
You'll have every failure, God; You'll have every victory.

You say I am loved when I can't feel a thing.
You say I am strong when I think I am weak.
You say I am held when I am falling short.
When I don't belong, oh, You say I am Yours.
And I believe, oh, I believe.
What You say of me.
I believe.

Oh, I believe, yes, I believe.
What You say of me.
I believe.

Artist: Lauren Daigle
Album: Look Up Child
Released: 2018
Genre: Christian/Gospel
Songwriters: Jason Ingram / Lauren Daigle / Paul Brendon Mabury
You Say lyrics © Sony/ATV Music Publishing LLC
Nominations: GMA Dove Award for Pop/Contemporary Recorded Song of the Year
Awards: GMA Dove Award for Song of the Year 2019; Billboard Music Award for Top
Christian Song 2019; Grammy Award for Best Contemporary Christian Music Perfor-
mance/Song 2019

Let go and let God

In 1990 I was 18 years old. I took a trip, with a bunch of friends from church, to Lake Arapuni, one of New Zealand's most beautiful North Island lakes. Long and narrow, Lake Arapuni is a drawcard for boaties and water-skiers.

We camped next to the lake and spent our daylight hours skiing and relaxing. One day, late in the afternoon, we decided to take the boat out for one more joyride. Six of us piled in, while the remaining four of our group stayed on the shore to fire up the BBQ.

The lake had been glass-calm all day, but – on this final trip – the wind had risen, and the surface had become choppy.

The old, wooden ski-boat was blasting along when it hit something just below the surface (which we can only assume was a log). The object broke through the bottom of the hull and water began to pour in. The driver, and owner of the boat, looked at us all and said: *"everybody out, it's going down."* No one in the group was wearing a life jacket, and I remember saying to the driver that I couldn't swim. There was one, tiny, rectangular floatation device in the boat. He could have kept it for himself, but he gave it to me.

Once we were in the water, fully-clothed, the turbulence separated us away from each other. I stayed as close as I could to two people, but, for all I knew, the others had disappeared and could have drowned.

I managed to remove the sweatshirt that was dragging me down, but my water-logged jeans were not helping with flotation. I do recall desperately trying to stop my grandmother's eternity ring from leaving my hand (it's funny the things that become important in a time of crisis).

We were too far from land, and the water was too strong for us to swim. We would see our friends as small coloured dots, far down the shoreline. We could also see another boat that was anchored around a bend in the lake, though we could not see anyone on-board.

The three of us who had remained together (my two companions treading water and me struggling to stay afloat on my floatation device), tried to yell "*help*" as loud as we could. Our land-based friends, afterwards, told us that they noticed the boat had not returned, and they thought they heard what sounded like cows mooing, but could see neither us nor any cows.

Finally, our efforts paid off, and we saw a pair of fluorescent orange and black beach shorts running down the beach. We were able to point him in the direction of the anchored boat, and around 20 minutes after pitching into the water, all six of us were rescued.

The reason that I tell you this story is that I genuinely thought I was going to die. It is one of two times in my life that I have been prepared to meet God face-to-face, and I know what it feels like to be inches away from the end.

Something important happened to me that day, which I want to offer as an encouragement for you in your walk with God. From the moment I saw water rushing in the bottom of the boat, I was terrified. I knew I couldn't swim, and so I struggled in my own strength to stay afloat. I battled in my head to think about what I could do in that situation, and how I could save myself, and I came up with nothing. There was absolutely nothing I could have done to keep myself alive at that point. So I decided to stop struggling and focus on God. The minute I relaxed and started to pray, things changed. My spirit calmed, my head cleared, and we saw the anchored boat.

LETTING GO

How often do you try to do things in your own strength? It can be tiring, can't it?

'Let go and let God' has become a beloved saying. When we feel overwhelmed, this phrase reminds us to give control over to God. It's a feel-good statement, but how accurate is it? If you, like me, have needed God to rescue you, support you or help you out, you may be wondering what it means to 'let go', and what part you should continue to play as you 'let God' do His thing.

There are two parts to this phrase: our part, and God's part. We need to figure out what we are letting go of and what we are letting God do. First, let's look at three things we should let go:

1 **Let go of control.** When I was in the lake, I had to stop relying on myself and recognise that I had no power over the waters and no means of gaining control at that moment. It's relatively easy to let God 'do His thing' when you are in a situation that is out of control. It's more challenging to let go if you are a competent person who maintains good order in their everyday life and relies on their own abilities to solve problems. In cases like this, letting go can sometimes be a test of how prideful we are.

   God has full knowledge and control of situations around us (*"Your Father knows what you need before you ask him."* Matthew 6:8, NIV). He knows the small and everyday situations as well as the big, unexpected ones. His part is to allow us to rest in His strength. Your part is to submit to His will and trust Him, even if chaos swirls around you.

2 **Let go of entitlement.** As part of God's family, you may think you are 'entitled' to various things, and that God (as your Heavenly Father who loves you) should bless anything and everything you may wish to do. We all hold fast to our dreams and expectations, believing that people should automatically act a certain way toward

us, and that life should oblige us and bend to accommodate our needs. To achieve all this, we expect that God should honour our wishes. However, being our Heavenly Father who loves us, He will always (without fail) want the BEST for us, not just agree with whatever we want, and that may mean God will say "no". God's part is to desire and design the best for us; our part is to put our wishes before Him and say "this is what I would love to do, but – ultimately – your will be done" and then graciously (and without sulking) accept His answer.

3 **Let go of worry.** In this decade, we are learning that nothing in our lives is immune to being shaken. We watch as the world is hit by one global epidemic, financial crisis or natural disaster after another, with the resulting loss of health, jobs, security, and even lives. As we pivot to cope with these changes, we can experience times of great anxiety, panic and depression if we don't maintain a healthy, godly perspective. For some people, it doesn't take a cataclysmic event, and they will worry about happenings in their everyday lives.

Worrying shows that we are doing one or both of two things: (1) that we are living in fear; or (2) that we are trusting in ourselves to solve a situation, and not trusting God.

The Bible repeatedly tells us "do not worry" and "do not fear." God's promises offer supernatural peace amidst financial challenges, sickness and family struggles – they can cut through the darkness where chemical sanitisers cannot.

God's part is to do what He says He will do in His Word – be our provider, healer, protector, shepherd and peace-giver. Our part is to let Him.

My continued existence is a testament that God does help. In my case, assistance came at the perfect time and incredibly quickly – at the point where I asked for it. You just have to believe and trust that God not only CAN help you but that the mighty creator of heaven and earth WANTS to help you and WILL help you.

HOW DOES LETTING GO HELP YOU AND YOUR PURPOSE?

"Hold loosely to the things of this life, so that if God requires them of you, it will be easy to let them go." (Corrie ten Boom)

I love this quote by the well-known Christian author, Corrie ten Boom, and I've tried to follow her words in my own walk – God needs you to hold things in your life and ministry loosely.

Along your purpose-led journey, God will ask you to do many things. If you are the type of person who holds onto things tightly (both tangible and intangible) or if you like to maintain firm control in your life, then it becomes difficult to let those things go or let God take over when He asks.

When Simon and I decided to move to Israel, in 2006, we owned our own home in the Bay of Islands, New Zealand, and had filled that home with lovely things that represented a lifetime of memories. I was also running a successful graphic design business that I had been building for eight years to that point.

We did not know how long God was taking us to Israel for, or where He might lead us after our work there was complete. The cost of storing a house-load of furniture and items for an indefinite time was prohibitive, so we closed my business, sold the house and almost every possession we had and left New Zealand.

If I hadn't been able to hold our material possessions 'lightly', it would have been a huge mental and emotional struggle to leave them behind and focus on doing what God wanted us to do. As it was, we were able to enter Israel unencumbered by 'things' (apart from our two dogs), which was surprisingly quite liberating.

Moving effectively in God's purpose for your life requires getting out of your own head; flexibility; obedience; sacrifice; willingness and an open heart. What a joy (and relief) it is when we can finally let go and let God!

"I have finally learned to turn off my head and let the Holy Spirit help me get out of my own way.

"I come from a pretty strong faith background and believe everyone has a purpose. All I want to do, while I'm on this planet, is align with my higher purpose, to ensure I make the dent I'm meant to make.

"In going to Burberry, I finally gave it up. I said, "lead me, guide me, show me." I begged for signs of clarity. So I tried to turn off my brain. Then, one day, if something is meant to be, I'll wake up, and it's as clear as day that I need to do this. I have tremendous faith, and that gives me the courage to let go in order to move forward, and – hopefully – be able to make a greater impact in my short time here."

(Angela Ahrendts, former Senior Vice President of Retail & Online Stores, Apple; from '*Extreme You*' by Sarah Robb O'Hagan)

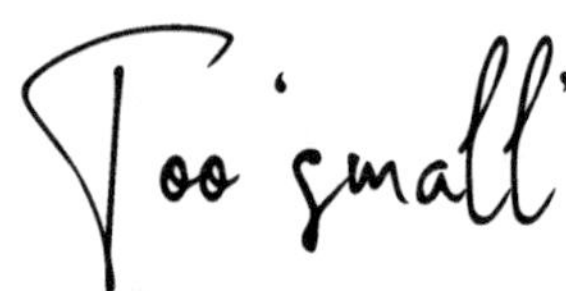

"Great things are done by a series of small things brought together."
(Vincent van Gogh)

A friend of mine, who we will call Hayley, is a really good mother. Actually, lots of people are really good mothers, but Hayley is a GREAT mother. Everyone knows it, and anyone who talks with Hayley for even a short time can sense a strong nurturing spirit emanating out of her.

Hayley grew up on a farm, attended a small rural school, and describes her youthful personality as 'reserved' and not particularly confident or outgoing. When I asked Hayley what she loved to do as a child, she said that she adored playing with dolls and 'playing house'. Hayley said that she always wanted to create a homely environment, even when she was playing outside.

When I asked Hayley what she loves to do now, as an adult, she said that she loves to spend time with her family (parents, husband, children and grandchildren), and to take care of the needs of others. Hayley has a strong pastoral gift, which she is able to outwork through her life at home, and through her local church.

When describing her gifts, Hayley seemed to suggest that her contribution to the world was 'small' or 'insignificant' and I was stunned.

There is nowhere in the Bible (that I have been able to find) that says God expects us to make a big, brassy contribution to the world on His behalf. Did you know that the 'rich', 'famous', 'awarded', 'beautiful' people get those descriptions because of what man thinks of their achievements? God would far rather use a description like 'obedient', 'gracious', 'faithful', 'diligent' and 'loving', and (in the interests of eternity) I know which words I'd rather be known by!

What I love about Hayley's story is that she is an excellent example of how God works out His purpose in a person's life. God gave gifts to Hayley (which I'm guessing to include pastoral, helps and mercy) which showed themselves strongly from a very young age. She acknowledged and embraced those gifts, even if she didn't realise what they were at the time.

You then add into the mix Hayley's gentle, caring personality and the environment that she grew up in (where she had stellar parental role models illustrating what it meant to care for others). All that remained was to see how God would outwork the assignments that He had for her throughout her life, and those assignments have centred around both her biological family and her church family.

Can you see the parallels that have existed throughout Hayley's life? Those are no coincidences! Her life is an exciting and clear example of God's intricate and predestined plan.

Sometimes we can get discouraged when we hear the 'big' or 'grand' stories of Christians doing prominent work; who may be amazing speakers or teachers; or those who are well-known in the church or the media. At other times we may look at certain gifts as being 'better' or 'bigger' than others, and if we don't have that particular gift, then we feel less significant.

There have also been some Christian preachers and teachers who use extreme examples to showcase how people walking in the Holy Spirit have done amazing, supernatural things. These examples are likely to be 100% true and wonderful, but they may not be the experience of everyone who walks in God's will and purpose. If we only look at those particular examples, they can skew our idea of what is 'normal' or 'usual'.

Our God cares about the small as well as the big. He loves all of His creation and has fashioned each one of us individually and intentionally for our individual paths.

There will be some Christians who will have prominent ministries and assignments, where they might heal the sick or raise the dead – but that is their life, and you are living your life, and it is a wasted exercise to try and compare the two.

As we will look at in **Step 7: Your world**, your purpose is not to make an impact on <u>the</u> world, it's to make an impact on <u>your</u> world, and in there is a subtle, but very important difference.

Too 'big'

In the Bible (Judges 6–8), we read the story of a man named Gideon. Gideon was a military leader, prophet and the fifth judge (renowned as the greatest) of Israel. Gideon is also included as one of the great men of faith listed in Hebrews 11. Let's take a look at how God first called Gideon into service for Him.

*"Now the angel of the Lord came and sat under the terebinth at Ophrah, which belonged to Joash the Abiezrite, while his son Gideon was beating out wheat in the wine press to hide it from the Midianites. And the angel of the Lord appeared to him and said to him, "The Lord is with you, O mighty man of valour." And Gideon said to him, "Please, my lord, if the Lord is with us, why then has all this happened to us? And where are all his wonderful deeds that our fathers recounted to us, saying, 'Did not the Lord bring us up from Egypt?' But now the Lord has forsaken us and given us into the hand of Midian." And the Lord turned to him and said, "Go in this might of yours and save Israel from the hand of Midian; do not I send you?" And he said to him, "Please, Lord, how can I save Israel? Behold, **my clan is the weakest in Manasseh, and I am the least in my father's house**." And the Lord said to him, "But I will be with you, and you shall strike the Midianites as one man." And he said to him, "If now I have found favour in your eyes, then show me a sign that it is you who speak with me. Please do not depart from here until I come to you and bring out my present and set it before you." And he said, "I will stay till you return."* (Judges 6:11–18, ESV, emphasis added)

In this passage about Gideon's calling, we can see (from Gideon's timid response) how he felt less-than-adequate to face the task put before him. I love the simple answer that the angel of the Lord gave to Gideon: "*I will be with you*".

Remember God's friend, Moses? God spoke to him and said "*So now, go. I am sending you to Pharaoh to bring my people the Israelites out of Egypt.*" (Exodus 3:10, NIV). And how did Moses reply? He said "*Pardon your servant, Lord. Please send someone else.*" (Exodus 4:13, NIV). He tried to back-pedal out of his assignment FIVE times! Even the mightiest men in the Bible – those who God tasked with seemingly impossible responsibility – had their doubts and insecurities.

Can you imagine saying "*no*" to God? Yet we do it all the time. Have you ever felt a prompting to pick up the phone and call someone? Or relay a difficult message? Or do something that pushes you outside your comfort zone? How many of those times did you follow through on the promptings? How many times did you walk away?

It's highly probable that God will give you an assignment or calling (or even a simple task) that you feel is bigger than you can handle, or something you don't want to do. That's called stretching your spiritual muscle!

If God asks you to do something, then He already has confidence you will be able to see it through (even if you can't see it yourself), and he's not about to set you a task then let you flounder. From the first page to the last, the Bible is chock-full of examples of God's provision and enablement.

Here's an encouraging word from Peter Mortlock (City Impact Church, New Zealand): "*God will give provision for your vision. He will provide. You can then relax and have peace in God. If you have a small vision, you will receive small provision, if your vision is big, then be assured that God will supply all you need.*" Amen to that!

Too young? Too old?

WHAT DO THOSE WORDS MEAN?

Have you ever been told (or felt) that you were either 'too young' or 'too old' to be moving in God's purpose and plans for your life? These phrases are limiting and destructive lies that Satan likes to pull out of his arsenal of tricks.

Before we uncover what God has to say about these two mindsets, let's pick apart the actual words for a moment.

The word 'too' can mean that something is either 'excessive' or that it has reached a greater degree of what is permissible, acceptable or possible. To know that something (in this case, you) has gone beyond the boundary of acceptability, you first have to know what that something (you) is being compared to.

When it comes to the phrases 'too young' and 'too old' we need to establish the baseline of acceptability from somewhere. I can guarantee you that there is not one single Bible verse or biblical proclamation that will tell you the ages when you can and cannot serve God. Therefore, which yardstick are you using to determine if you or someone else is 'too young' or 'too old'? The only possible answers are that you are listening to your society, culture, family, or peers. Perhaps you are making a personal judgement call based on your upbringing or experiences. Maybe you are letting your fears dictate your destiny.

Fortunately for everyone, when you are living a Bible-believing life with a heart after the things of God, then He will use a different measuring system to decide if the time is right for you.

Now that we understand that we are talking about concepts that do not exist in God's vocabulary let's dig deeper.

'TOO OLD'

It has been written that there are seven stages of human life: infancy, early childhood, middle childhood, adolescence, early adulthood, middle adulthood and old age.

Modern Western culture has developed an unfortunate attitude toward those who sit in the 'old age' stage of life. Society will tell you that as a person's age increases there comes a perceived decline in physical attractiveness, the ability to perform everyday tasks, and the ability to learn new things. Families seem more inclined to pack their senior members off to a rest home than to keep them under the same roof as an esteemed member of the extended family unit.

On the upside, there can also be a perceived increase in wisdom, knowledge, and respect (more notable in some cultures than others).

If your head listens to the opinions of the world and you choose to accept that you are 'too old', then your heart will close off to the plans that God has for you. When God looks at you, He doesn't notice wrinkles or a slower gait. The Bible records a conversation between God and Samuel, where God himself says: "...*for the Lord sees not as man sees: man looks on the outward appearance, but the Lord looks on the heart.*" (1 Samuel 6:7, ESV). Therefore, who are you choosing to listen to and believe – the world or God?

The Bible records two instances of women who were barren and who society considered to be 'too old' to give birth to a child – Sarah (Genesis 18) and Elizabeth (Luke 1).

God had His own plans, and both of these women became mothers to two of the most venerated people in Biblical history – Isaac and John the Baptist. Both births happened at just the right time in history to fulfil God's big picture plan.

If God can work a miracle to allow a person past child-bearing age to have a child, what miracle or unexpected thing do you think He could do in your life? You are NEVER too old to begin a new assignment. If it is an assignment from God, then He will be with you along the way and give you all the strength and support you will need.

There are some assignments that only someone of advanced years could do, or where an older person is required to be relatable or exhibit age-related empathy, or be able to reach out to particular people. Age should also come with a measure of wisdom and experience.

My late mother, Pam, lived until she was 83 years old. In 2007 doctors gave her an estimated three months to live, and she lasted a further 2^1/2 years.

During the final phase of her life, she was confined to a bed in a medical rest home with a diagnosis of cauda equina syndrome (CES), which led to permanent paralysis. Along with CES, breast cancer had metastasised throughout her body, which reduced her ability to move the muscles in her face and limbs.

There were times, throughout this long, slow process of facing her mortality that my mother wondered what she was doing and why God had not yet taken her away. Why did she linger when she couldn't do anything, go anywhere or even barely talk?

Though my mother's body was failing, her mind remained sharp, and she retained her ability to speak until right at the end of her time.

We had no clarity around God's intentions for her, and could only guess. I would try to encourage her to look for small opportunities each day to bless the people she came in contact with – the nurses that fed her, bathed her and cared for her. Mum's body was failing, but she could still give a slight smile or a word of encouragement. Maybe she was there to be the ray of sunshine in someone's day.

It is also possible that my mother's end-of-life assignment was to teach me something (such as compassion) or to be able to use her experience to help someone else (like in a book that I might write 14 years after her passing). We may never know the whys and wherefores. All we can do is to be faithful to God and to live out our days in the most kingdom-minded way we can.

Breath = life = purpose. God knows exactly the number of days that you have been apportioned. You can, therefore, logically conclude that if God has not yet taken you home to be with Him, He still has at least one more assignment for you to do. Your task may be large, like Moses (at 80 years old) leading the Israelites out of Egypt, or something small such as well-timed words to someone who needs it most.

Sid Roth (prolific author and host of the TV and online show '*It's Supernatural*') once said that "*no demon in hell can take you out until you have fulfilled your destiny.*" It's now up to you to believe it.

'TOO YOUNG'

Judging whether a person is 'too young' to be moving in God's purpose is just as subjective as deciding if someone is 'too old'. It's easy to fall into the trap of putting our own experiences and biases onto the lives and callings of others (no matter their age), so it's important to bring our opinions back in line with Scripture to see what God says to us through His Word.

Through Scripture, we can gain an understanding of how God works in the lives of Believers and how age is literally just a number when someone has been given a particular calling or assignment.

Here are some biblical accounts of people who started their assignments at a 'young' age:

KING JOSIAH

We read about King Josiah in our section on predestination. In 1 Kings 13:1–2, we discover that Josiah's reign and works were prophesied 300 years before his birth and we can continue reading about Josiah in 2 Chronicles 34: 1–7 (ESV):

"*Josiah was eight years old when he began to reign, and he reigned thir-*

ty-one years in Jerusalem. And he did what was right in the eyes of the Lord, and walked in the ways of David his father, and he did not turn aside to the right hand or to the left.

"For in the eighth year of his reign, while he was yet a boy, he began to seek the God of David his father, and in the twelfth year, he began to purge Judah and Jerusalem of the high places, the Asherim, and the carved and the metal images. And they chopped down the altars of the Baals in his presence, and he cut down the incense altars that stood above them. And he broke in pieces the Asherim and the carved and the metal images, and he made dust of them and scattered it over the graves of those who had sacrificed to them. He also burned the bones of the priests on their altars and cleansed Judah and Jerusalem.

"And in the cities of Manasseh, Ephraim, and Simeon, and as far as Naphtali, in their ruins all around, he broke down the altars and beat the Asherim and the images into powder and cut down all the incense altars throughout all the land of Israel. Then he returned to Jerusalem."

Josiah was only 8 years old when God providentially set him on the throne of Judah. His father had been wicked, as had the Jewish kings and culture for generations before him.

The key to Josiah's success and notability can be found in verse 2: *"And he did what was right in the eyes of the Lord, and walked in the ways of David his father; and he did not turn aside to the right hand or to the left."* In the years when Josiah was stepping into adulthood (aged 16+ years old), his heart responded wholly to the Lord.

TIMOTHY

Timothy was born in the Lycaonian city of Lystra in Asia Minor (modern-day Turkey). He was born of a Jewish mother, Eunice (who had become a Christian believer), and a Greek father. The Apostle Paul met him during his second missionary journey, and he became Paul's companion and co-worker along with Silas.

Through the course of his preaching, Paul calls Timothy not only *"a true son in the faith"* (1 Timothy 1:2, NKJV), but also his *"brother and minister of God, and our fellow labourer in the gospel of Christ."* (1 Thessalonians 3:2)

Paul and Timothy went for extended periods living away from each other, and so they communicated via letter. We are blessed to have many of Paul's letters recorded in the Bible, including two specifically written to Timothy.

Tradition has it that Timothy was around 16 years old when he and his Jewish mother were converted to Christianity, and around 21 years old when he joined Paul and Silas on Paul's second tour through Asia Minor.

In 1 Timothy 4:12–16 (NIV), Paul sends Timothy the following words of encouragement:

"Don't let anyone look down on you because you are young, but set an example for the Believers in speech, in conduct, in love, in faith and in purity. Until I come, devote yourself to the public reading of Scripture, to preaching and to teaching. Do not neglect your gift, which was given you through prophecy when the body of elders laid their hands on you.

"Be diligent in these matters; give yourself wholly to them, so that every-one may see your progress. Watch your life and doctrine closely. Persevere in them, because if you do, you will save both yourself and your hearers."

Timothy, even as a young man, was recognised as an elder in the church because of his spiritual development and knowledge of God's divine plan.

In this short passage, Paul gives us several tips for those who have received a clear assignment and calling from God at an early stage in their life:

- ***"Don't let anyone look down on you because of your age"***. Don't accept their words. Don't let the opinions of others be a cause of discouragement for you.

- ***"Set an example for the Believers"***. Be an example of uprightness, integrity and morality for others – no matter your age, and despite your age.

- ***"Do not neglect your gift"***. If you know that God has bestowed a particular gift on you, then you should use it (wisely).

- ***"Be diligent in these matters…so that everyone may see your progress"***. Diligence is having or showing care and conscientiousness in your work or activities. It's a trait that is not typically demonstrated by those who are young, and so it is a powerful way for you to stand up and stand out from those around you.
- *"**Watch your life and doctrine closely. Persevere in them.**"* A 'doctrine' is a set of beliefs. If your doctrine is based on Scripture and godly principles, then watch out that the ways of the world do not sway you from your path and principles. Persevere (continue), even when things get difficult or discouraging.

JEREMIAH

And, lastly, we'll read another passage about the life of the prophet, Jeremiah.

Jeremiah was one of the four major prophets in the Old Testament of the Bible, along with Isaiah, Ezekiel and Daniel.

In Jeremiah 1:6–8 (NIV), Jeremiah writes:

"Alas, Sovereign Lord," I said, "I do not know how to speak; I am too young." But the Lord said to me, "Do not say, 'I am too young.' You must go to everyone I send you to and say whatever I command you. Do not be afraid of them, for I am with you and will rescue you," declares the Lord."

We know from the beginning of the book of Jeremiah that he started his ministry in the thirteenth year of the reign of King Josiah of Judah, which was 627 BC (Josiah's reign began around 641 BC).

Opinions vary about the year of Jeremiah's birth, but there is a consensus that Jeremiah was between 13 and 20 years old when the Lord called him as a prophet to the nation of Judah, and Jeremiah continued to serve the Lord for the rest of his life.

God does a great job of summing up how to tackle life as a 'young' person with a divine calling. Firstly, don't worry about the fact that you are young in the eyes of the world – age is immaterial from God's perspective. Simply be willing to do what He tells you to do and say what He wants you to say. In return, He promises that He will be with you and is there to help you along the way!

Too flawed

Are you embarrassed or ashamed of your past? Are your failures holding you back? If there was such a thing as a 'sin scale' for your life, would your needle be sitting squarely in the red zone? Do you dearly hope that there is a godly purpose for your life, but shrink away, wondering how a person like you could ever be used for God?

There is a passage in the Bible known colloquially as the 'Faith Hall of Fame'. It was written by the Apostle Paul and can be found in Hebrews 11:4–38 (NIV). I'd like for you to read the whole passage, as we will learn one very important thing at the end. Here goes:

FAITH AT THE DAWN OF HISTORY

"By faith, Abel offered to God a more excellent sacrifice than Cain, through which he obtained witness that he was righteous, God testifying of his gifts, and through it he being dead still speaks.

By faith, Enoch was taken away so that he did not see death, "and was not found, because God had taken him"; for before he was taken he had this testimony, that he pleased God. But without faith, it is impossible to please Him, for he who comes to God must believe that He is and that He is a rewarder of those who diligently seek Him.

By faith Noah, being divinely warned of things not yet seen, moved with godly fear, prepared an ark for the saving of his household, by which He condemned the world and became heir of the righteousness which is according to faith.

Faithful Abraham

By faith, Abraham obeyed when he was called to go out to the place which he would receive as an inheritance. And he went out, not knowing where he was going. By faith he dwelt in the land of promise as in a foreign country, dwelling in tents with Isaac and Jacob, the heirs with him of the same promise; for he waited for the city which has foundations, whose builder and maker is God.

By faith, Sarah herself also received strength to conceive seed, and she bore a child when she was past the age because she judged Him faithful who had promised. Therefore from one man, and him as good as dead, were born as many as the stars of the sky in multitude – innumerable as the sand which is by the seashore.

The Heavenly Hope

These all died in faith, not having received the promises, but having seen them afar off were assured of them, embraced them and confessed that they were strangers and pilgrims on the earth. For those who say such things declare plainly that they seek a homeland. And truly if they had called to mind that country from which they had come out, they would have had opportunity to return. But now they desire a better, that is, a heavenly country. Therefore God is not ashamed to be called their God, for He has prepared a city for them.

The Faith of the Patriarchs

By faith Abraham, when he was tested, offered up Isaac, and he who had received the promises offered up his only begotten son, of whom it was said, "In Isaac, your seed shall be called," concluding that God was able to raise him up, even from the dead, from which he also received him in a figurative sense.

By faith, Isaac blessed Jacob and Esau concerning things to come.

By faith Jacob, when he was dying, blessed each of the sons of Joseph, and worshipped, leaning on the top of his staff.

By faith Joseph, when he was dying, made mention of the departure of the children of Israel, and gave instructions concerning his bones.

The Faith of Moses

By faith Moses, when he was born, was hidden three months by his parents, because they saw he was a beautiful child; and they were not afraid of the king's command.

By faith Moses, when he became of age, refused to be called the son of Pharaoh's daughter, choosing rather to suffer affliction with the people of God than to enjoy the passing pleasures of sin, esteeming the reproach of Christ greater riches than the treasures in Egypt; for he looked to the reward.

By faith, he forsook Egypt, not fearing the wrath of the king; for he endured as seeing Him who is invisible. By faith, he kept the Passover and the sprinkling of blood, lest he who destroyed the firstborn should touch them.

By faith, they passed through the Red Sea as by dry land, whereas the Egyptians, attempting to do so, were drowned.

By Faith They Overcame

By faith, the walls of Jericho fell down after they were encircled for seven days. By faith, the harlot Rahab did not perish with those who did not believe when she had received the spies with peace.

And what more shall I say? For the time would fail me to tell of Gideon and Barak and Samson and Jephthah, also of David and Samuel and the prophets: who through faith subdued kingdoms, worked righteousness, obtained promises, stopped the mouths of lions, quenched the violence of fire, escaped the edge of the sword, out of weakness were made strong, became valiant in battle, turned to flight the armies of the aliens. Women received their dead raised to life again.

Others were tortured, not accepting deliverance that they might obtain a better resurrection. Still, others had trial of mockings and scourgings, yes, and of chains and imprisonment. They were stoned, they were sawn in two, were tempted, were slain with the sword. They wandered about in sheepskins and goatskins, being destitute, afflicted, tormented — of whom the world was not worthy. They wandered in deserts and mountains, in dens and caves of the earth."

Let's consider some of the most well-known, inspiring, godly individuals who the Apostle Paul singled out for special mention in the 'Faith Hall of Fame'. At certain points in their life, the world would have viewed the following people like this:

- Noah was a drunkard.
- Abraham was a liar and didn't trust God to follow through on His promise.
- Sarah was a doubter.
- Jacob was a liar, cheater and manipulator.
- Moses was a murderer.
- Rahab was a prostitute.
- David was a liar, adulterer and an accessory to murder.
- And to cap it off, the writer of the passage, Paul himself, persecuted Christians and was an accessory to murder.

Every single one of us has a 'past'. Every single one of us is flawed. As you can see, even some of the most revered, God-fearing, Bible-believing Christians committed awful, unconscionable sins during their lifetime.

Fortunately for all of us, our loving God looks at people differently than the world does. For those who choose to leave their past behind them, turn to God and walk the path that He lays out for them, then He will wash their slate clean. The Bible says *"as far as the east is from the west, so far has He removed our transgressions* [sins] *from us."* (Psalm 103:12, NIV). That is such a precious promise!

OK, what if you believe that your sin is REALLY bad. Can it be worse than murder? Remember that Moses was a murderer, and both David and Paul devised or sanctioned the murder of innocent people. We know, from Scripture, that *"if we confess our sins, he is faithful and just and will forgive us our sins and purify us from all unrighteousness."* (1 John 1:9, NIV). That's ALL unrighteousness, not just certain sins over others, and that includes all your past actions.

Of course, some of our sins will have permanent consequences, and – no matter what our current relationship is like with God – we will have to accept the consequences of our actions. When confronted by Nathan for his adultery and murder, David confessed and repented. Nonetheless, the child born to Bathsheba died, and David's family dysfunction continued.

God can use any of us, regardless of our past, if we will lean on him in faith (just like these Hall of Famers) and step out in obedience to do what He asks us to do.

The Believers of history were imperfect, weak and needy. But God, in His great mercy, revealed Himself and His strength despite their weaknesses. In the same way, God does not require your strength, because he knows you don't have any! He delights in moulding you by His intentional, compassionate handiwork and bringing you eternal joy.

As we read in Hebrews 11, it is faith that pleases God. Not your performance. Not your results. Not your good works. Not a perfect track record. Not what others think of you. Faith; and faith alone.

ALL THINGS WORK TOGETHER FOR GOOD

There is a saying that 'a person's greatest heartache can become their greatest ministry'. God will often use your past experiences as part of your greater purpose here on earth. Now, that's not saying that God deliberately caused you to sin, or experience pain and hardship to further His glory or Kingdom - that's not in God's nature at all. However, what He does like to do is take all the rubbish in our lives, compact it together, then turn it around for good.

Often there are things that you will go through, which will make you more compassionate towards others who have experienced similar situations. For example, perhaps you have spent time in prison; have had a miscarriage; grew up in an abusive home; or have been through a divorce. There are hurting people out there who need someone – just like you – who can speak into their lives. Not everyone will be able to relate to their experiences, but maybe you can.

As you work your way through the *Purpose Discovery Wheel*, think about every aspect of your life, even the parts you would prefer to forget. It's often in those areas where God can use you the most.

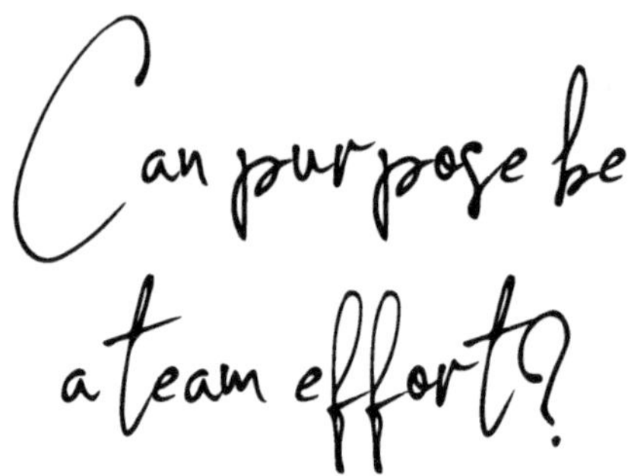

One question that was racing around my head when I first started writing this book was *can two or more people share the same purpose?* The short and easy answer is "*no*". As we now know, God has made us each of us 100% unique individuals, and this uniqueness extends through to the purpose and plans that He has for your life.

However, there is no reason why two people can't share a similar 'fire', calling or assignment. Let's look at the story of Ronni Kahn, the Founder and CEO of OzHarvest (OzHarvest.org). The following is a transcript of Ronnie speaking at the AANA conference in Sydney, Australia, 2019.

"I thought "what can I do?" My skill set was really about putting on events. I was an event producer; I had a business that was working with some major corporates. At every one of my events, the thing that was most obvious (and the best way to engage and connect people) was around food. Food shows generosity and abundance and prosperity, so all of my events had a massive amount of food, and that meant that there was [usually] a mass of food [left over].

When I could, I would take that food and deliver it to an agency on my way home. It was pretty confronting, stepping over a lot of men going to Matthew Talbot [a shelter and support service provider for homeless men in central Sydney]. *I'd step over these people and hand over my tray.*

I started thinking that perhaps I could do that better. I knew there was food, and I knew there were people in need. What was important was that I saw there was a gap. [In the gap] was something I needed – if someone could have taken my food and delivered it, that would have been so cool, but there wasn't, so I needed to do that.

For some of you who are thinking about how you could make a difference in your little worlds or big worlds, think about what it is that you know, what it is that [hacks] you off, what it is that irks you. When you find the solution to that, the chances are that other people had that same problem.

It turns out that actually, collecting surplus food and giving that food to people who needed it was quite a good thing!

It took a year to get OzHarvest up and running. I do recall that when I decided that this was what I wanted to do that I was like a woman possessed and I thought it would take a month. I thought I'd make a few phone calls, phone some of the rich people that I knew whose events I had been doing. I would share with them that I needed some money because I needed a telephone and an office and a truck, and they'd give it to me. And I'm still waiting for some of them to return my calls! However, I realised that if it took me for the rest of my life, I now knew what it was that I needed to do.

In November 2004 our first van left our office, and it had written on it "Rescuing Food for the Charities of Sydney". I pinched myself black and blue because I had created what I wanted to do. In that first month, we collected and delivered the equivalent of 13,000 meals and delivered it to six charities. I can't even tell you how it felt.

Last month, we delivered the equivalent of 825,000 meals to 585 different charities around Australia, and it feels extraordinary, and I now know what it feels like to make an impact on people. But I want to share with you that I could not do this by myself and I haven't done it by myself. I have an extraordinary team of people.

OzHarvest is like a magnet for magnificent people.

It's up to each and every one of us to do something significant, and significant doesn't have to be huge. Significant is about making a difference to somebody as often as you can. I want to share with you that it's way more rewarding, and giving is a thousand times better than getting."

SOMETHING BRAND NEW OR EXISTING?

Ronnie Khan followed the 'fire' that was burning inside her and created a charity that now blesses the needy of Australia with millions of meals each year.

I don't know if Ronnie is a Christian or what beliefs she holds. She felt compelled to start a new endeavour from scratch, and you can see the apparent blessing that is on the OzHarvest initiative.

If God is telling you to start a new endeavour, then He will equip and support you to do it. However, you should know that you don't need to create something brand new for you to outwork your God-given purpose.

Due to the nature of the OzHarvest charity, and how it closely aligns with Christian principles, there is a high chance that Ronnie will have several Christian people working within her team. As Ronnie said herself, OzHarvest is like a "*magnet for magnificent people*", where like-minded, like-hearted people flock to help build the work she is doing. Do all these people share the same life-purpose as Ronnie? No, not at all. But each of those people will be able to contribute their own blend of skills, talents, gifts, personality and 'fire' to help propel the endeavour forward.

LIVING SOMEONE ELSE'S PURPOSE

Simon and I were married in 2001, and for the lion's share of these past 20+ years I honestly felt that my life's purpose was to support my husband, Simon. I couldn't see any particular strength or specialness in my gifts or what I could offer the wider world as I didn't understand how God's purpose worked for individuals. What I did see was a clear call on Simon's life, and so my natural assumption was that God had put me on this earth to be a help-mate for him and his calling.

The biggest mental hurdle that I had to get over was to do with where my gifts could be used. I grew up with the incorrect belief that gifts and talents are given for use solely within the local church or some form of 'Christian ministry'. Whilst that is true to a certain extent, it is only part of the story as *Purpose Made* will help to unfold.

I knew I had solid skills in particular areas, but I thought they were all work-related and not church-related. I spent years despairing that I did not have a 'Christian ministry' and feeling like I didn't 'fit' anywhere in a spiritual context. It has only been in recent years that I have looked at the concept of purpose afresh, through God's eyes, and understood what that means for me.

Your God-given purpose is yours – not your spouse's, not your mother's or father's, not your child's; it's yours alone. Can you ride the coat-tails of someone else's purpose? Yes, it's easy to do that. Should you? No. There may be some areas which dovetail nicely together, and if there are then that's great – that means that God has purposefully planned it that way.

When I look at our marriage now, I can see how God has united two very different (though highly-complementary) people. We each have a different combination of gifts, different personalities, different callings and different assignments. The outworking of our God-given purposes is also extremely different.

However, I know without a doubt that God knew exactly what He was doing when He brought us together. He knew that we would off-set each other and lend strengths to the other's weaknesses; light to the other's shadows; and balance to the other's personality. Along with the differences, we also share similar world views, similar beliefs, and similar tastes.

If I had continued in my thinking that I would merely share in Simon's purpose, then my life would have been woefully incomplete, and the people around me would have lost out on the blessings that I can bring. I may have done the support job well, but my purpose would have remained dormant and unfulfilled, and the resulting discontent would most likely have affected our marriage. Thankfully, I caught my misunderstanding in time, and my individual, one-of-a-kind purpose is now firmly back on track!

Purpose Discovery Wheel

Introduction

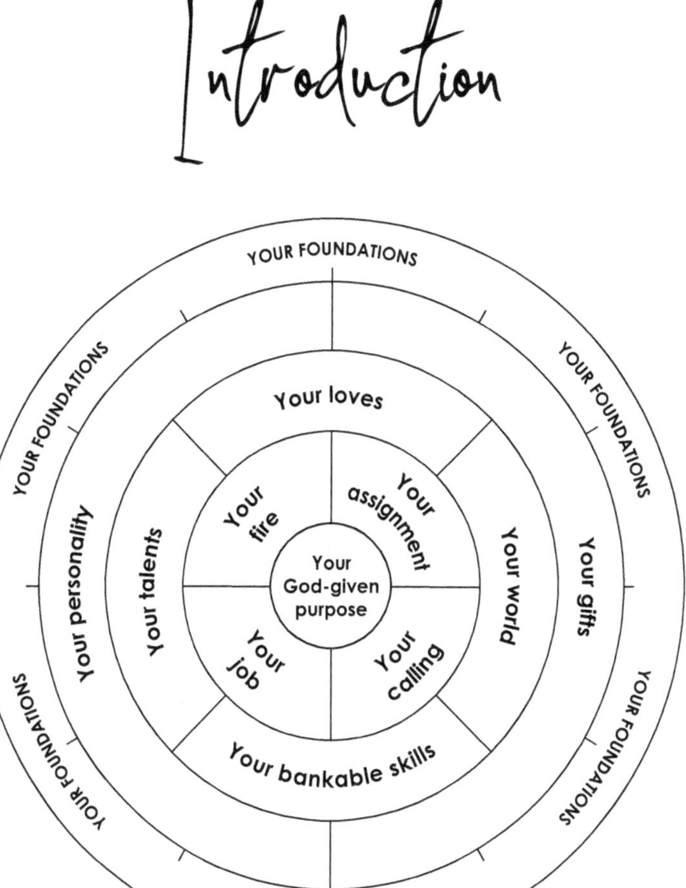

"Therefore, I urge you, brothers and sisters, in view of God's mercy, to offer your bodies as a living sacrifice, holy and pleasing to God – this is your true and proper worship. Do not conform to the pattern of this world, but be transformed by the renewing of your mind. Then you will be able to test and approve what God's will is – his good, pleasing and perfect will." (Romans 12:1–2, NIV)

One of the beautiful things to come out of preparing this book for you is that I have watched people go through the *Purpose Discovery Wheel* process, and end up beaming at the other end.

Time and again, a person will receive a revelation of their purpose (or calling, or gifts) that they say they always sensed was there, but never realised what significance it all meant in God's greater plan for their lives, or never knew what to do with what they had been given.

The thing about purpose is that God has intentionally wired you a certain way. There will be traits you exhibit without thinking or natural inclinations that you have that can serve as strong clues to your God-given purpose.

Our responsibility is first to recognise how God has wired us, which should then help you better understand your next steps. The *Purpose Discovery Wheel* process will help you to do just that.

Before we start, let's look at what God revealed to Clare Jones, the creator of the *Life Without Limits* programme at City Impact Church, New Zealand:

"I used to feel so bad that I never just loved everybody. [Instead,] I could always see the thing, in somebody, that needed fixing.

"I would spend, honestly, years on my knees every night repenting, "Lord, I am just so sorry that I don't love everybody like you love them." And I repented, and I repented, and finally, one day, God said to me (almost) "for crying out loud, it's a GIFT I've given you! Stop repenting of it! It's a gift I've given you to help the person, so then when they talk to you, you can say "hold on, have you thought about this, or thought about that?" Sometimes

we are repenting for gifts!

"The funny thing is that God has brought me, over the years, full-circle. I wanted to love everybody; then I realised He had given me a gift of seeing what we could do to help (here is a problem and issue and here is the solution). Now I've come around full-circle because now I do, I love the person! Instead of repenting, I recognise it."

The *Purpose Discovery Wheel* is all about clarifying your God-given purpose and illuminating God the Father's good, pleasing and perfect will for your life. We will do this by working our way through the following 12 steps:

1   Your foundations
2   Your personality
3   Your gifts
4   Your talents
5   Your loves
6   Your bankable skills
7   Your world
8   Your 'fire'
9   Your job
10 Your calling
11 Your assignment
12 Your God-given purpose

There are certain facets of the *Purpose Discovery Wheel* that may change little throughout your life, such as your personality, gifts, loves and talents. Other aspects will most certainly change, such as your job, your bankable skills, your world and your assignments. Plus, there are facets that God may choose to reveal over time and in accordance to your walk with Him, your maturity and the condition of your spiritual muscle. These facets may include your 'fire', your calling and your purpose.

Therefore, it's a good idea to go through these 12 Steps every few years to review how God has been speaking to you, guiding you and revealing your purpose in greater depth.

There are no wrong answers for any step in this process – what God has placed within you can never be wrong! Your task is to recognise the wheat from the chaff, and then weed out anything in your life that is not of God so that you can give the right and good aspects of your life a chance to take root, grow and become fruitful.

The *Purpose Discovery Wheel* is a tool to help you make sense of your special, unique and complex life and figure out the "why am I like I am?", "what's it all for?", "where do I fit in?", and "what should I do next?" questions.

Let's get this wheel rolling!

STEP 1

Your foundations

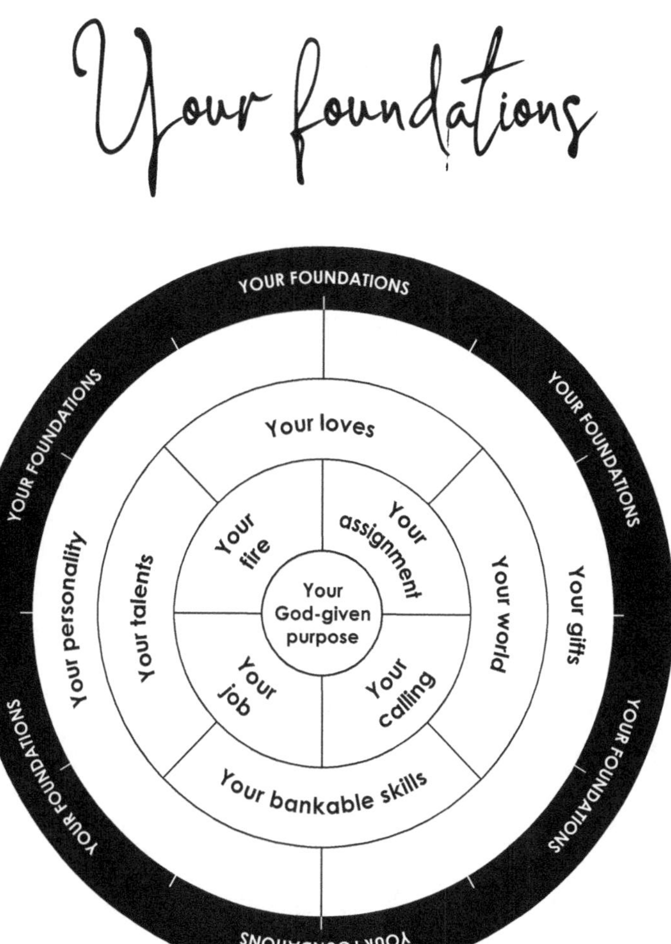

"He who kneels the most stands the best."
(D.L. Moody)

You are about to embark on a potentially life-changing journey to discover God's purpose and plan for you, and so you need to ensure that you build your foundations in a right and godly manner.

Every journey has to have a starting point, and you will find yours in the Bible, in Proverbs 16:1–9 (ESV). The following passage was written by King Solomon, the wealthy and wise son of King David, who ruled over the nation of Israel from around 970 BC to 931 BC.

Solomon's words sum up the importance of prayer when it comes to figuring out the path that we should walk in life.

- **Proverbs 16:1.** *"The plans of the heart belong to man, but the answer of the tongue is from the Lord."*

  It's super-easy to make choices and plans and execute them in your own strength. Our mind can be a swirling mass of ideas, and it can be challenging to decipher what our thoughts and plans are versus what is God wanting us to do. It is comforting to know that the ultimate *"answer of the tongue"* (the last word) is from God, and we can rely on Him to have the correct answer in our particular circumstance…every single time.

- **Proverbs 16:2.** *"All the ways of a man are pure in his own eyes, but the Lord weighs the spirit."*

  Just because something seems 'pure' to do (or right or logical or timely), it doesn't mean it's the best thing for you right at this moment. The Lord will be able to judge your "spirit", and what's motivating you.

- **Proverbs 16:3.** *"Commit your work to the Lord, and your plans will be established."*

That's a powerful promise from God and one that you can hold fast to when things look murky or stagnant.

Here's another powerful verse that dovetails nicely with Proverbs 16:3, "*do not be anxious about anything, but in everything by prayer and supplication* [seeking/asking] *with thanksgiving let your requests be made known to God.*" (Philippians 4:6–7, ESV)

God cannot carry out His work through a heart that is anxious, disobedient (sinful), fearful or if you are doing something for your own glory. The best way to assure that your plans will be successful is to dedicate your ways and works to God and be willing to say, "Thy will be done", then allow Him to guide you in your walk.

- **Proverbs 16:4.** "*The Lord has made everything for its purpose, even the wicked for the day of trouble.*"

Even the wicked (both people and plans) will eventually become subservient to God's purposes. For example, even Pharaoh (whom we read about earlier in the story of Moses) through his rebellion and hard-heartedness could not change God's plans for the deliverance of His people. In fact, Pharaoh's responses only gave God more occasions to show His power, justice, goodness and patience.

- **Proverbs 16:5.** "*Everyone who is arrogant in heart is an abomination to the Lord; be assured, he will not go unpunished.*"

How often do we choose to take matters into our own hands in the effort to speed things up, or to get some traction going? Is it not arrogance to think that we know better than God does himself? As if we could out-think or out-manoeuvre the God who created the entire universe! Personally, I have no wish to be considered an "abomination to the Lord", so I'll do what I need to do to keep God in the driver's seat of my decisions, and prayer is a great way to start!

- **Proverbs 16:6.** "*By steadfast love and faithfulness iniquity is atoned for, and by the fear of the Lord one turns away from evil.*"

The Bible often says that we need to have a healthy *"fear of God"*, which can be a bit confronting when we read the word 'fear' with our modern minds. Fearing God doesn't mean that we should be 'afraid' of Him, it means that we should be in awe of His holiness, to give Him complete reverence and to honour Him as the God of great glory, majesty, purity and power.

We need to recognise that God is loving, merciful and forgiving; but he is also holy, just and righteous. Knowing God (and understanding his character) means accepting the fact that his justice and holiness (and separation from evil) cause him to judge sin (our 'iniquities').

When it comes to asking God to bring light to our path and to show us the purpose and plan that He has for us, Proverbs 1:7 (ESV) says *"The fear of the Lord is the beginning of knowledge."* That's great news and gives us the starting point of our journey.

- **Proverbs 16:7.** *"When a man's ways please the Lord, he makes even his enemies to be at peace with him."*

This is another powerful 'when/then' promise that we can declare – one where we have a condition to fulfil before we get the reward. WHEN we are walking according to God's Word (the Bible), in a Christ-like manner and with faith, THEN even our enemies will be at peace with us. That promise will come in mighty handy as we seek to live out God's purpose for our lives.

- **Proverbs 16:8.** *"Better is a little with righteousness than great revenues with injustice."*

If you think that walking in God's purpose for your life will be the ticket to receiving great earthly riches (as it was with Solomon, the author of these Proverbs), then now will be a good time to reset those thoughts.

We read (in the section 'Too flawed') about the 'Faith Hall of Fame' in Hebrews 11. The Apostle Paul celebrated the heroes and martyrs who made up the fabric of our Christian history. What made them distinctive was not how much money they had, but how obedient they were to God's plan for their lives. In fact, of those who suffered the most, the scripture says in Hebrews 11:38, *"the world was not worthy of them."*

Better by far is it to live as it suggests in Proverbs 30:8 (NIV), *"give me neither poverty nor riches, but give me only my daily bread"*, and seek to walk in righteousness in all that we do.

- **Proverbs 16:9.** *"The heart of man plans his way, but the Lord establishes his steps."*

Here we circle back around to the sentiment in verse 1. You can and should plan your way, but in everything, commit your plans to God in prayer; let Him know what you are thinking; ask Him to give you the wisdom that you need, to know what to do and where to go.

Like it says in an earlier Proverb, also written by Solomon, *"trust in the Lord with all your heart, and do not lean on your own understanding. In all your ways acknowledge Him, and He will make straight your paths."* (Proverbs 3:5–6, ESV)

Let's summarise Step 1 in the journey to discover your purpose. Your foundations should be:

- Don't burden yourself with anxiety or worry.
- Have healthy awe and reverence (fear) of God, your creator.
- Trust in Him with all your heart.
- Talk (pray) to God about all your plans, questions, frustrations, hopes and dreams; ask him to give you wisdom and understanding.
- Be aware of how God speaks to you, then allow Him the room to respond to your prayers and guide you.

Then, if you do all these things, God says that He will "make straight your path", which is an exciting thought and leads us onto Step 2 on the *Purpose Discovery Wheel*.

Purpose Discovery Wheel

STEP 2

Your personality

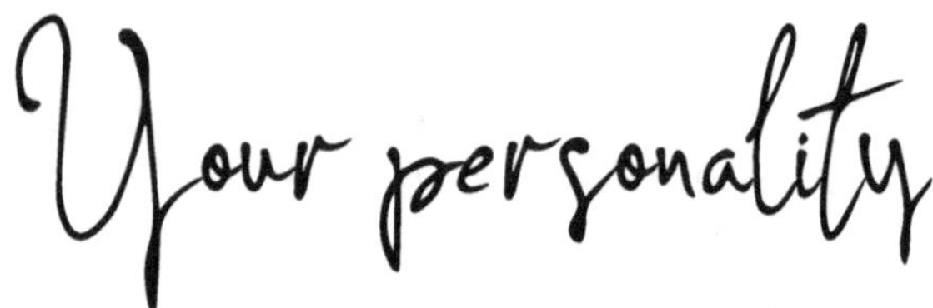

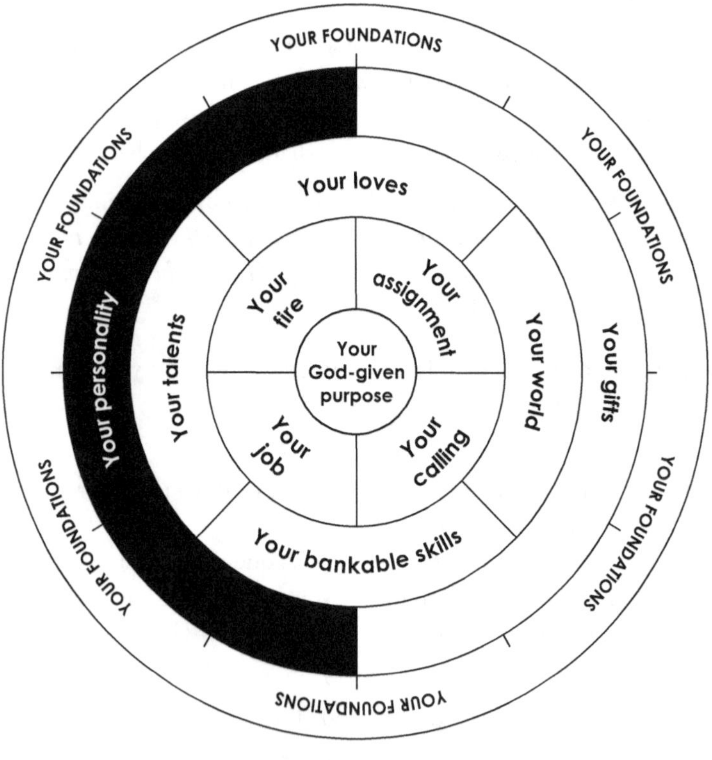

DEFINITION OF 'PERSONALITY'

- The combination of characteristics or qualities that form your distinctive character.
- Your nature, disposition, and temperament.
- Your personality may be shaped and refined over the years, but will likely stay fairly consistent throughout your life.

What characteristics make up your personality?

Let's look at this question in three parts.

Part 1: Write down all the words you can think of that describe your personality:

____

____

____

____

____

____

____

____

Part 2: Ask one or two people (who know you well) to describe your personality and write down what they say. It can be beneficial to choose one family member and one friend (or a colleague) to obtain different perspectives.

____

____

____

____

____

____

____

____

____

Part 3: Take an online personality test* and write down the key personality traits that the test reveals. Indicate [agree / disagree] whether or not you agree with the test results for each trait. It's a good idea to print or take a screen shot of your results so you can refer back to them in the future, or paste them into this book with the date you took the test.

____ agree / disagree

____ agree / disagree

____ agree / disagree

____ agree / disagree

____ agree / disagree

____ agree / disagree

____ agree / disagree

____ agree / disagree

____ agree / disagree

____ agree / disagree

____ agree / disagree

EXAMPLES OF FREE ONLINE TESTS:

- 16personalities.com (a modified, free version of the MBTI test, below) - provides a particularly comprehensive report.
- High5Test.com
- Crystalknows.com/personality-test

EXAMPLES OF PAID ONLINE TESTS:

- MBTI (Myers-Briggs Type Indicator): MBTIonline.com
- Gallup CliftonStrengths Assessment: Gallup.com/cliftonstrengths

Please note that I have no personal affiliation to any of these websites, and the website links were current at the time this book was published.

A personality test should only confirm what you already know about yourself, but it may package the results in a way that is illuminating or interesting for your reference.

Most personality tests will classify you into a 'type', which can then lead to some people feeling like they have been put into a 'box', generalised and categorised. Personality tests are extremely broad, and so you will, inevitably, find some results that you agree with and other results that you feel do not fit you at all. That's normal, and you should hold any test result that you receive very lightly and objectively.

PERSONALITY vs HEART

The Bible has very little to say about personality traits, which is a strong indicator that 'personality' (in of itself) is not of great importance in the scheme of life. We can infer from the omission of information that our interest in personality traits has come more from man's desire to understand how different people tick, rather than what God thinks of the matter.

Instead, we read a lot about the condition of the 'heart' (this is metaphorical, not physical!), which Scripture regularly uses as an analogy to describe a person's intellect, emotions, will and the centre of their conscience.

If you are interested in reading more about what the Bible says about the heart, here are some verses for you.

THE HEART IS OUR INTELLECTUAL CENTRE
- Heart and mind are closely linked: Philippians 4:4-8, Mark 2:8
- We can hide the Word of God in our heart: Psalm 119:11
- Perception is a function of the heart: Matthew 13:14–15

THE HEART IS OUR EMOTIONAL CENTRE
Several emotions spring from our heart, including:
- Love: Matthew 22:37
- Anxiety: John 14:1, 27
- Peace: Philippians 4:7

- Gladness and sincerity: Acts 2:46, Ephesians 6:5
- Evil thoughts: Matthew 15:19
- Pride: Psalm 131:1

THE HEART IS THE LOCATION OF OUR WILL
- Obedience: Romans 6:17, Ephesians 6:6
- Belief: Romans 10:9
- Decisions: 2 Corinthians 9:7

THE HEART IS THE LOCATION OF OUR CONSCIENCE AND MORAL AWARENESS
- The law of God is inscribed on our heart: Romans 2:15
- We are aware of eternal values: Ecclesiastes 3:11
- Our conscience can be corrupted: 1 Timothy 4:2

WHERE DOES PERSONALITY FIT IN?

My take on the lack of scriptural reference to 'personality' is that our different personalities are so normal and natural to God that they are – in essence – unremarkable. That's great news, given how vastly different we all are!

I can also infer that this silent endorsement means there are no 'right' or 'wrong' personality 'types'. All personalities are equal – no one type is better than any other. Therefore, the goal of defining your personality type is simply to better understand yourself, and better understand and appreciate the differences that exist between people.

The more important task is to ensure that the condition of your (metaphorical) heart stays healthy so that the way you conduct yourself outwardly (your personality) is wholly pleasing to God.

God knew and predestined precisely the type of personality that you would have. As you make your way through the 12 Steps of the *Purpose Discovery Wheel* you will see how perfectly your personality fits in with God's plan for your life and the assignments that He has mapped out for you.

I can guarantee that every single one of your unique characteristics will come in handy along your equally-unique journey ahead.

STEP 3

Your gifts

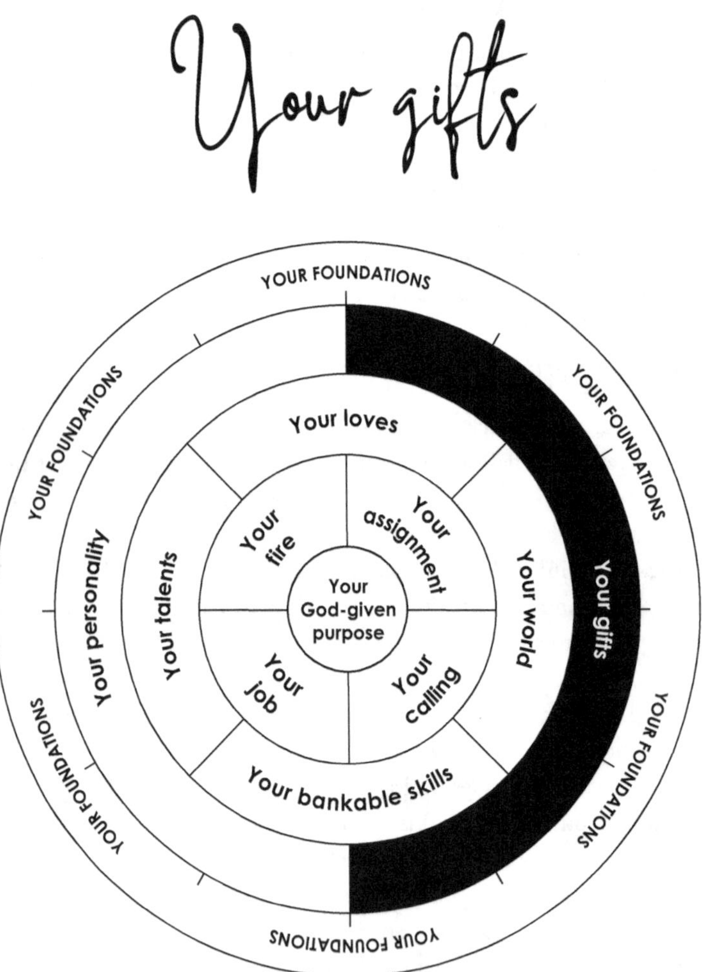

"The meaning of life is to find your gift. The purpose of life is to give it away."
(Pablo Picasso)

You may have noticed that I have titled Step 3 of the *Purpose Discovery Wheel* 'Your gifts' rather than 'Your Spiritual gifts'. Many people, within the church, often refer to all gifts as 'Spiritual gifts' whereas the Bible talks about three distinctly different types of gifts, which we will cover here (one of those types being 'Spiritual gifts').

Being able to identify your gifts helps you to more clearly see what you can do to serve and edify (build up) others – primarily within the ekklesia, or Body of Christ (a.k.a. the church), but also for the outworking of your God-given assignments and broader purpose.

Knowing your personality and gifts will help you to identify how you can serve others. Then, understanding the 'fire' that drives you, your calling and what your assignment is (which we will cover in Steps 8, 10 and 11), will help to identify where you are best suited to serve.

Your gifts were never meant to be locked away for safe-keeping or kept safe for a rainy day. They have been given to you as a way to glorify God and to bless others, and those are verbs – action words. They are outward-focused, not inward-focused. To stretch your spiritual muscle, you need to start using the gifts that you have been given; and to use your gifts, you first have to figure out what they are!

It's also vitally important that you have an overview of all the gifts so that you understand how your gift(s) can fit in with the rest of the gifts that are (or should be) operating within the Body of Christ (the church).

The Apostle Paul lists all the gifts over three letters contained in the Bible – to the churches in Rome (in Romans 12), Ephesus (in Ephesians 4), and Corinth (in 1 Corinthians 12). If you look closely at the three mentions about gifts in Paul's letters, you can see that each set has been given to us by either God the Father, Jesus Christ, or the Holy Spirit.

Let's read each of the passages to identify the gifts and see how they fit into our lives as individuals and as part of the Body of Christ.

GOD-GIVEN GIFTS (A.K.A 'GRACE GIFTS' OR 'MOTIVATIONAL GIFTS')

The following is an excerpt from a letter that Paul wrote to the church in Rome, found in Romans 12:4–8 (NIV):

"For just as each of us has one body with many members, and these members do not all have the same function, so in Christ we, though many, form one body, and each member belongs to all the others. We have different gifts, according to the grace given to each of us. If your gift is prophesying, then prophesy in accordance with your faith; if it is serving, then serve; if it is teaching, then teach; if it is to encourage, then give encouragement; if it is giving, then give generously; if it is to lead, do it diligently; if it is to show mercy, do it cheerfully."

Here Paul highlights seven God-given gifts:

1 **Prophecy**. Edifies, exhorts and consoles the church by reporting something that God spontaneously brings to your mind.
2 **Service**. Can also be translated as 'ministry'; gives service to the church in one or more of the many ministry areas.
3 **Teaching**. Having a special ability to instruct others and communicate God's Word in effective ways.
4 **Encouragement**. Also known as 'exhortation'; the ability to motivate and bolster Believers, to comfort and help them in times of need.
5 **Giving**. Sharing your possessions with others with above-and-beyond generosity.
6 **Leading**. Having a people or project leadership role which could include things like administration, financial management, and strategic planning.
7 **Mercy**. Having a ministry of visitation, prayer and compassion.

These God-given gifts are often referred to as 'motivational gifts'. When you contemplate which of the gift(s) you may have been given, think about what 'motivates' you.

For example, in my life, I have been given gifts of encouragement, leading and teaching. My strongest motivation is to encourage other people (both in my work life and church life). This motivation is bubbling under the surface all the time, and I can't suppress it. A lot of what I do (in my conversation, writing and business initiatives) is underpinned by a desire to build people up and strengthen them.

What motivates you? Which of these gifts can you recognise operating in your life?

JESUS-GIVEN GIFTS (A.K.A THE 'FIVE-FOLD MINISTRY')

In Ephesians 4:11–16 (NIV) the Apostle Paul writes specifically about equipping gifts.

"So Christ himself gave the apostles, the prophets, the evangelists, the pastors and teachers, to equip His people for works of service, so that the Body of Christ may be built up until we all reach unity in the faith and in the knowledge of the Son of God and become mature, attaining to the whole measure of the fullness of Christ.

"Then we will no longer be infants, tossed back and forth by the waves, and blown here and there by every wind of teaching and by the cunning and craftiness of people in their deceitful scheming. Instead, speaking the truth in love, we will grow to become in every respect the mature body of Him who is the head, that is, Christ. From Him, the whole body, joined and held together by every supporting ligament, grows and builds itself up in love, as each part does its work."

Paul lists five gifts, given to us by Jesus Christ specifically for the equipping of the church:

1 **Apostle.** A messenger; one sent forth with orders; commissioned to initiate and direct the preaching of the gospel.
2 **Prophet.** Equips the church for works of service through exhortation, edification and consolation.
3 **Evangelist.** Devotes themselves to preaching the gospel.

4 **Pastor**. Can also be translated as 'shepherd'; one who leads, guides and sets an example for other Believers.

5 **Teacher**. Devotes themselves to preaching and teaching the Word of God.

You will notice that each of these gifts are designations or titles, rather than a reference to the works they perform (such as 'mercy' or 'helping'), which makes these gifts particularly unique.

Jesus Christ intended that ALL five people-giftings (not just one or two) are required to equip His people for service so that the Body of Christ (the church) becomes mature, strong and bonded together. The five gifts are often referred to using a hand analogy, because of the power of the five fingers working together.

One important thing to note is only certain Believers will operate in these Jesus-given gifts, so if you feel that you don't 'fit' into one of the five-fold ministry roles, do not despair. Jesus Himself selects specific people to fill these roles within the Body of Christ, and this designation will dovetail in beautifully with that person's other gifts, calling, assignments and overall purpose.

HOLY SPIRIT-GIVEN GIFTS

In Paul's letter to the church in Corinth (1 Corinthians 12:1–26, NIV), we read about the *"gifts of the* [Holy] *Spirit"*, which we also call 'Spiritual gifts'. Paul writes in detail about how each gift has its place within the Body of Christ (the church).

"Now, about the gifts of the Spirit, brothers and sisters, I do not want you to be uninformed. You know that when you were pagans, somehow or other you were influenced and led astray to mute idols. Therefore I want you to know that no one who is speaking by the Spirit of God says, "Jesus be cursed," and no one can say, "Jesus is Lord," except by the Holy Spirit.

"There are different kinds of gifts, but the same Spirit distributes them. There are different kinds of service, but the same Lord. There are different kinds of working, but in all of them and in everyone it is the same God at work.

"Now to each one the manifestation of the Spirit is given for the common good. To one there is given through the Spirit a message of wisdom, to another a message of knowledge by means of the same Spirit, to another faith by the same Spirit, to another gifts of healing by that one Spirit, to another miraculous powers, to another prophecy, to another distinguishing between spirits, to another speaking in different kinds of tongues, and to still another the interpretation of tongues. All these are the work of one and the same Spirit, and he distributes them to each one, just as he determines.

"Just as a body, though one, has many parts, but all its many parts form one body, so it is with Christ. For we were all baptised by one Spirit so as to form one body – whether Jews or Gentiles, slave or free – and we were all given the one Spirit to drink. Even so the body is not made up of one part but of many.

"Now if the foot should say, "Because I am not a hand, I do not belong to the body," it would not for that reason stop being part of the body. And if the ear should say, "Because I am not an eye, I do not belong to the body," it would not for that reason stop being part of the body. If the whole body were an eye, where would the sense of hearing be? If the whole body were an ear, where would the sense of smell be? But in fact God has placed the parts in the body, every one of them, just as he wanted them to be. If they were all one part, where would the body be? As it is, there are many parts, but one body.

"The eye cannot say to the hand, "I don't need you!" And the head cannot say to the feet, "I don't need you!" On the contrary, those parts of the body that seem to be weaker are indispensable, and the parts that we think are less honourable we treat with special honour. And the parts that are unpresentable are treated with special modesty, while our presentable parts need no special treatment. But God has put the body together, giving greater honour to the parts that lacked it, so that there should be no division in the body, but that its parts should have equal concern for each other. If one part suffers, every part suffers with it; if one part is honoured, every part rejoices with it."

To summarise, the nine gifts given to us by the Holy Spirit and according to God's grace (a.k.a. Spiritual gifts) are:

INSIGHT GIFTS:

1 **Wisdom**. Speaking by the Spirit of God, which manifests some part of God's total wisdom for the direction of the Body of Christ.
2 **Knowledge**. Speaking by the Spirit of God, which manifests some part of God's total knowledge for the information of the Body of Christ.
3 **Distinguishing between spirits**. Also called 'discernment of spirits'; the capacity to discern, distinguish or discriminate the source of a spiritual manifestation.

POWER GIFTS:

4 **Faith**. Having a strong and special faith (such as can move mountains or cast out demons), as distinguished from the 'saving' or 'normal' faith of a Believer.
5 **Healing**. The ability to supernaturally minister healing to others.
6 **Miraculous powers**. Also known as 'miracles'; the performance of deeds beyond ordinary human ability, by the power of the Holy Spirit.

SPEAKING GIFTS:

7 **Prophecy**. See previous.
8 **Speaking in tongues**. The supernatural ability to speak an unlearned language; Paul advises that the private use of this gift is for the spiritual strengthening of oneself and that the public use of this gift must always be interpreted.
9 **Interpretation of tongues**. This gift always follows the public exercise of the gift of tongues.

These gifts have been given to people who believe in God and can say that Jesus is Lord (verse 3). They are special abilities given to Believers to glorify God, to edify others and for the common good and unity of the church body.

THE 'GREATER' GIFTS

Here is an important passage of Scripture that follows on immediately from the passage about Spiritual gifts, and can be found in 1 Corinthians 12:27–31 (NIV).

"Now you are the Body of Christ, and each one of you is a part of it. And God has placed in the church first of all apostles, second prophets, third teachers, then miracles, then gifts of healing, of helping, of guidance, and of different kinds of tongues. Are all apostles? Are all prophets? Are all teachers? Do all work miracles? Do all have gifts of healing? Do all speak in tongues? Do all interpret? Now eagerly desire the greater gifts."

Whoa, now we are talking about *"greater gifts"*! What does the Apostle Paul mean by that? This passage singles out nine specific gifts:

1 **Apostle**. See previous.
2 **Prophet**. See previous.
3 **Teacher**. See previous.
4 **Miracles**. See previous.
5 **Healing**. See previous.
6 **Helping**. Having a spiritual burden and a God-given love for the needy and afflicted.
7 **Guidance**. Also known as the gift of 'governing' or 'administration'; the ability to steer, lead, guide or be a helmsman for the Body of Christ.
8 **Kinds of tongues**. See previous.
9 **Interpretation** [of tongues]. See previous.

All the gifts listed in verses 1–26 are good and desirous and divinely-given, but Paul highlights the nine gifts above as being the *"greater gifts"*, and includes mention of gifts that he wrote about in his other letters. He does that, not to belittle some gifts, but to encourage Believers to desire after the gifts that are more essential than others – those that focus on the greatest welfare of the church body.

In the same breath, Paul also cautions that we cannot all be apostles, prophets, workers of miracles or have gifts of healing and that our ambitions for the 'greater gifts' should not lead to envy or resentment which can only cause division in the Body of Christ. The very next chapter in 1 Corinthians 13 is all about love, where Paul reminds us that we should strive to outdo one another in love, and it is love that underpins all the gifts.

MOSES AND HIS GIFTS

I love the story of Moses (which we read earlier) as it gives us wonderful insight into a life full of purpose, and a clear indication of what gifts can look like when they are outworked.

Let's filter Moses through the seven God-given gifts of Romans 12 to see which gifts he would have had. Remember that these gifts are given "*according to the grace given to us*" (of which Moses would have been given a lot!) and include **prophecy**, **service**, **teaching**, **encouragement** (exhortation), **giving**, **leading** and **mercy**.

PROPHECY

We are told that the gift of prophecy is given according to the portion of our faith, and Moses' faith had taken a hit in his first 40 years.

Until the age of 40, and growing up as an Egyptian prince, Moses would have had a high opinion of himself. When he realised that his people (the Hebrews) didn't accept him, he would have felt rejected and humiliated. After murdering an Egyptian man, Moses fled to the land of Midian.

His next 40 years, living in Midian, would have been a time of humbling, so when God called Moses at 80 years old (via his experience with the burning bush), Moses likely felt a level of reluctance and a realisation that he could not do things in his own strength. But this was exactly the time when Moses' gift of prophecy kicked into gear.

Moses asked for (and was granted) his brother, Aaron (the priest), to act as his mouthpiece. God gave Moses prophetic words and messages for the Pharaoh and the Hebrew people, which were then communicated by Aaron.

SERVICE

Moses is often cited as a biblical example of servant leadership. He demonstrated a deep love for God and others; humility in his approach to God and his own abilities; an impetus to serve God, and His chosen people; compassion; altruism and stewardship.

Moses also demonstrated how important stewardship and empowering others is to the optimal functioning of a community or organisation.

Moses served God and the Hebrew people for the last 40 years of his life. He was totally dedicated (in every aspect of his life) to his people, and to the work that God had entrusted to him.

TEACHING

It is a traditional belief that the first five books of the Old Testament (which the Jewish people refer to as the 'Torah ') were written by Moses. The Hebrew meaning of the word 'torah' means 'teaching' and Moses is also traditionally referred to as the 'Great Teacher'.

In Acts 15:21 (NIV) we read *"for the law of Moses has been preached in every city from the earliest times and is read in the synagogues on every Sabbath."* This verse refers to the ancient Jewish custom of the Rabbi's special seat at the synagogue which is called the 'Moses' Seat'. Jesus himself reinforced this when He said: *"The teachers of the law and the Pharisees sit in Moses' seat."* (Matthew 23:2, NIV).

We know, from reading through the book of Exodus, that Moses regularly imparted God's messages, the Ten Commandments, and numerous laws, to all the Hebrew people. God had obviously blessed him with a gift of teaching.

LEADERSHIP (WITH DILIGENCE)

Moses was by no means a perfect human being, but his close relationship with God allowed him to guide a rebellious nation of people into relationship, identity and purpose as the chosen people of God.

Moses led the Israelites for 40 years. He had to have learned diligence as he learned leadership. He had to carry out the ten judgements (plagues) of God exactly as God intended. The one time he operated without diligence and did not carry out God's instruction as he should have (by striking the rock in the desert), showed some of the impulsive characteristics of Moses of his early years. As a result, he was not allowed to enter the Promised Land with the rest of his people.

There are ample stories from Moses' life that point to the virtues and outworking of his leadership gift.

While they may have been minor gifts in his life, Moses did not obviously display the gifts of encouragement (exhortation), giving or mercy.

WHAT ABOUT YOU?

When we read these passages from the Bible, it can all seem quite 'lofty', and you may be feeling a sense of *"but who am I?"* compared with those in the early church. Remember that Paul was living at exactly the same time as Jesus, so the churches received his letters within their first 30 years of being established – and they hadn't had the benefit of all the wealth of teaching and resources that we can claim today!

Be encouraged. The Apostle Peter wrote (in 1 Peter 4:10–11, NIV) that each Believer will receive at least one of the gifts: *"Each of you should use whatever gift you have received to serve others, as faithful stewards of God's grace in its various forms. If anyone speaks, they should do so as one who speaks the very words of God. If anyone serves, they should do so with the strength God provides, so that in all things, God may be praised through Jesus Christ."* That is a word for both the 1st Century church and the 21st Century church, and a word directly for you!

Peter also writes that the gifts can be broken down into speaking gifts and serving gifts. He gives us a warning that if we have a speaking gift, then we need to be aware we are speaking the very words of God (no pressure!), and if we have a serving gift, then we need to work in

God's strength, not in our own strength. We do this to give God the glory, not ourselves, and always for the benefit of others.

It is likely that when you read through the Bible passages about gifts, certain ones will resonate strongly with you, and you'll have a sense of certainty about the gift or gifts that you have been given.

If you would like to take an online test to better identify your gifts, then you could visit

gifts.churchgrowth.org/spiritual-gifts-survey/

and take the *Spiritual Gifts Survey**. It's a good idea to print or take a screen shot of your results so you can refer back to them in the future, or paste them into this book with the date you took the test.

*Please note that I have no personal affiliation to this organisation, and the website was current at the time book was published. The Spiritual Gifts Survey does not differentiate between God-given, Jesus-given and Holy-Spirit-given gifts, and – therefore – the list of gifts covered in the survey results is incomplete. However, the survey report should bring you some clarity, which you can put before God for confirmation.

Question

Knowing that you have been given at least one of the God-, Jesus- or Holy Spirit-given gifts, which gift(s) do you think is (are) yours, and is each one a speaking or serving gift?

____

speaking / serving

____

speaking / serving

____

speaking / serving

____

speaking / serving

____

speaking / serving

SAME GIFT, DIFFERENT JOURNEYS

A good friend of mine, who we will call Jackie, and I share two of the same God-given gifts – those of teaching and exhortation (encouragement). Therefore, one might think that our purposes would be similar, or that the way we outwork those gifts might follow the same path. However, our two shared gifts are where the similarity of our journey ends.

Jackie's set of gifts also includes mercy and shepherding, while my gifts round out with strength in administration. Jackie is people-focused, and I am task-focused.

Jackie has a heart for sharing the gospel and encouraging those who are sad, lonely or depressed. I have a heart for supporting people in business.

Jackie's assignments have been to help individuals in their personal and spiritual lives, while my assignments have been to help individuals in their professional lives.

We both teach – Jackie is a tutor for young people with special needs, and for adults learning English as a second language; I train people working in the digital, advertising and marketing industries. And we both encourage others using our different styles and personalities.

So, you see, you may share the same gifts with others, but your journeys will be quite different. When you combine your gifts with every other step in this *Purpose Discovery Wheel* (including your personality, the things you love, your career pathway, your assignments and what drives you forward), you will discover a culmination of factors which serve to highlight a God-given purpose that is totally unique to you. God has intended for you to have an impact on this world in a way that only you can fulfil, and that's an exciting and comforting thought.

BEWARE THE GREEN-EYED MONSTER

"A heart at peace gives life to the body, but envy rots the bones."
(Proverbs 14:30, NIV)

Have you ever found yourself envying the gifts or personalities of other people? I know I have. I spent much of my Christian walk envying friends who had been given the gift of mercy. People with this gift almost always have sweet, nurturing and compassionate natures (like Jackie), and I thought that having a super-caring spirit was a highly-attractive quality that I was missing. I remember the years of repeatedly praying to God to make me a softer and more compassionate person.

My gifts and personality are more the matter-of-fact-get-things-done-quickly-and-in-good-order type. While I like giving hugs, I'm not exactly the 'cuddly' type, and I'm pretty sure that no-one who knows me would ascribe the words 'soft' or 'sweet' to my list of attributes. Instead, they would probably describe me as 'determined', 'resilient' and 'decisive'.

It's only in recent years that I have come to understand that the tougher side to my personality is my strength and not my weakness. I know, now, that God has given me this 'edge' so I can push through the particular assignments that He sends my way. I just wish that I had known that earlier in my life and hadn't wasted so many years wishing I was someone else.

God has given each of us very specific gifts and personalities for a reason. When you envy others, you are not only minimising the precious gifts you have been given; you are also doubting God's wisdom, and implying that He somehow got your allocation and life-plan wrong.

If you truly believe the words of Jesus Christ when he said (in Luke 12:7. NIV) that *"the very hairs on your head are all numbered"*, then you need to acknowledge that God knows you better than you do yourself and that He knew what he was doing when he created you. He doesn't get things wrong. Ever. And that includes you.

MOVING FORWARD

Your personality and your gifts will underpin and be evident through all the other steps of the *Purpose Discovery Wheel*. Once you have finished the 12 steps, you will be able to look back and see how your gifts provide the structural support for the purpose that God has for your life.

I can guarantee that you will have an 'a-ha!' moment when you look at the various facets of your life through the lens of your gifts. You will see how God has not only predestined you for an amazing purpose but that He has also pre-equipped you to handle the tasks ahead. Our God is most certainly an awesome, caring and minute-detail-oriented God!

STEP 4

Your talents

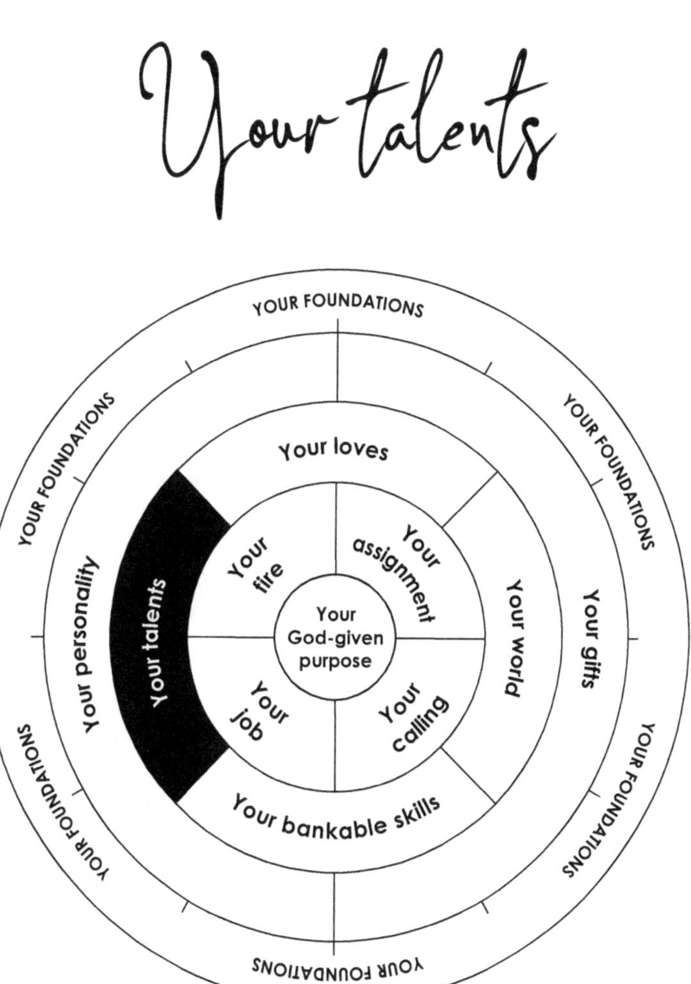

DEFINITION OF 'TALENTS'

- Talents can also be known as your 'skills' and 'abilities'.
- Your talents will likely develop over time as you become exposed to new experiences and activities.

What are your talents?

To help you answer this question, consider the following:

- What comes easily to you?
- What are you particularly good at doing?
- When are you most effective?
- What strengths or abilities do other people recognise in you? It can be helpful to ask your friends and family for their input – often others will see your talents more clearly than you can.
- What do people repeatedly compliment you on or remark about?
- Do you have any talents that were evident as a child or young adult?

After you have considered these questions, what are your top three to five answers? Are these talents you have had since a young age, or were they developed with time and practise?

____

young age / developed with practise

____

young age / developed with practise

____

young age / developed with practise

____

young age / developed with practise

____

young age / developed with practise

____

young age / developed with practise

NATURAL TALENTS

Have you ever heard the term 'naturally talented'? This is a common phrase people use to describe someone who exhibits skills and abilities with seeming ease – as though they came out of the womb already singing, dancing, climbing or leading. What mankind has conveniently ascribed to 'nature' we know better as coming directly from our creator God.

I am a great believer in the idea that God not only predestined you with a purpose, personality and gifts, but that he also gave you talents that he knew would help you with your journey.

When recognised and encouraged from a young age, these abilities can become a foundation stone for a person's purpose. It is, therefore, vitally important to recognise special interests and abilities in children and provide opportunities for those skills to grow.

BUT WHAT IF I'M MISSING SOMETHING?

As we discussed, earlier in this book, things like talents and skills can be heavily influenced by our life circumstances, the people around us and opportunities. The bottom line is that God knew exactly where, when and to whom you would be born. He knew everything that you would need in your toolbox to outwork the plans He pre-planned for you.

With that knowledge in mind, you can be confident that He has put the desire to learn and develop certain things within you, or He will bring the right people and opportunities your way to teach you what you need to know at just the right time.

If you have a heart after God and a desire to do His will, then He will make sure that you have all the talents you will need, packaged in a you-sized box.

STEP 5

Your loves

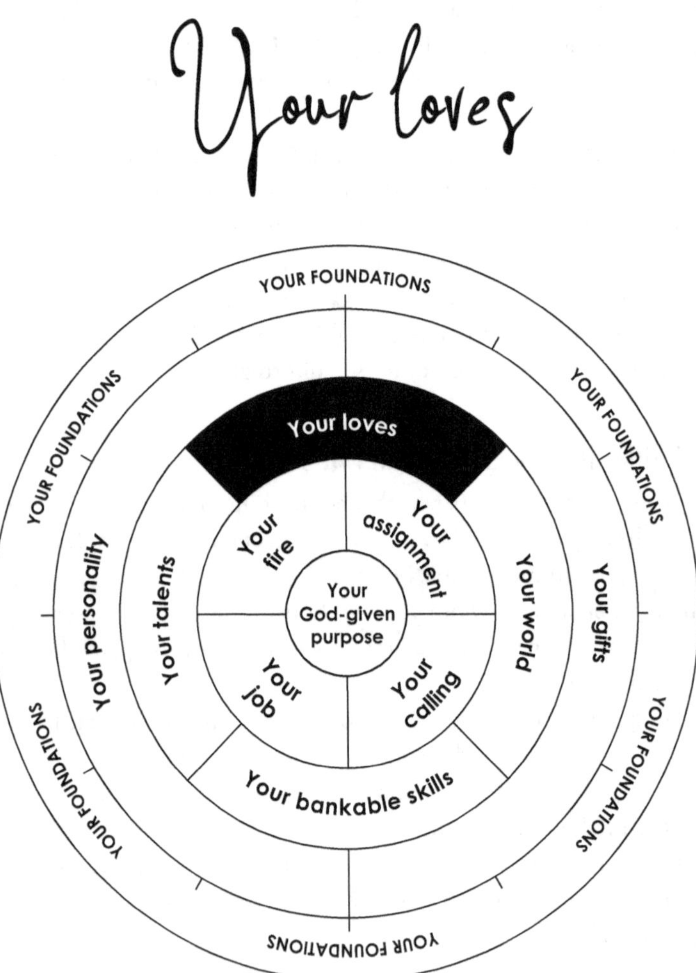

DEFINITION OF 'YOUR LOVES'

- Your loves could be people, animals, places, activities, causes or objects.
- If you are struggling to think of things you love, then start with things you really like.
- Your loves will develop over time as you become exposed to new people and experiences.

What are your loves?

To help you answer this question, consider the following:

- What makes you glow?
- When do you feel most 'alive'?
- What makes you feel happy?
- When were the times in your life that you experienced the greatest joy (a.k.a. your 'joy triggers')?
- What qualities do you enjoy expressing the most in the world? What ways do you enjoy expressing those qualities?
- What things, people, or activities do you spend the most time or attention on?
- What do you like spending your discretionary income on?

It's important to separate your 'loves' from your 'likes'. I 'like' a lot of different things, but there are only a few things in my life that I 'love'. Narrowing down what you love will help to bring you some clarity and make the rest of the *Purpose Discovery Wheel* easier to complete.

After you have considered these questions, what are your top three to five answers? Is there an underlying theme running through the things you love? If so, write that down too.

YOUR INBUILT GUIDANCE SYSTEM

Along with your conscience, 'gut feelings', your 'fire', and flight/ fight fear responses, 'joy' is also part of the internal guidance system that God has placed in your body to help you know when you are on the right path. Figuring out your 'joy triggers' can help to identify the things that you love most in life, and these have a strong bearing on our ultimate goal – finding your God-given purpose.

PUT THERE BY GOD

"If your kid beats on everything in your kitchen with sticks, he's probably

supposed to be a drummer. If your daughter dances over the house the whole time, she is probably supposed to be a dancer. You are supposed to make the way for them to be raised in those gifts – that's what God put on the inside of them. And then, when they are established – everyone in that arena where they use that gift – they can impact them for the gospel." (Kat Kerr)

Please don't ever think that the things you truly love doing are 'ungodly' just because they are not mentioned in the Bible. For example, if you like flower arranging, or bike riding, or restoring cars, then God can use you and your interests to reach other like-minded enthusiasts in a way that other Christians (with different interests) may never be able to do.

HEALTHY LOVES

The things you love may or may not become involved directly in the purpose that God has in store for you. What they are is a helpful indicator of the person that God created you to be.

God wants the best for your life, and that includes for you to have a healthy mind, body, soul and spirit. Monitoring the things you love helps to assess your heart-health (soul and spirit) and to see whether your focus is on the right things according to God's plan.

WHAT DO YOU TREASURE?

"For where your treasure is, there your heart will be also." (Matthew 6:21, ESV)

Another word to describe something that you 'love' is the word 'treasure'. If something is of genuine value to you, there's no disguising it. The worth you place on the various things in your life is evident by your priorities. Those things which mean the most to you will get the greater share of your time, attention and money.

That which you treasure (love), you treat like a treasure. When your idea of a treasure aligns with God's idea, then life-changing things can happen.

LOVES THAT MAY NOT LEAD TO YOUR PURPOSE

There may be some things you love that end up having nothing to do with your purpose, but they still contribute to making you you.

For example, I love, love, love writing. It's at the core of my being and couldn't stop writing if I tried. I know – without a doubt – that writing is a core part of my purpose, and I have and will use that love and ability to bless others.

On the other hand, I also love music, and this has been an integral part of my life from my earliest memories. I have a well-developed ability to remember words when put to a melody. When I was around 14 years old, I had a collection of over 500 song lyrics (which was an impressive number in pre-internet days), and I knew most of those lyrics by heart. To this day, I can still recall the words of songs that I haven't heard in decades.

My love of music has also manifested in my love of playing the piano. My mother, Pam, was a Grade 8 pianist, and so I grew up listening to her play tunes from classical to stage shows to pop. To her credit, my mother did try to teach me Grade 1-level practical and theory. I remember sitting in front of the keys, tapping out a few notes, then (being your typical, stubborn child) deciding that I didn't want my mother as my teacher, and so I spent the next 10+ years in piano-wasteland.

When I was about 20 years old, I bought myself a book of piano chords. I already knew how to read the treble line of music from many years playing woodwind instruments, so I just needed to teach my left hand what to do. As one piano teacher told me – 25 years later – I play "very well, and very poorly", but I play with gusto, and my cat doesn't mind.

The irony of being able to remember all those lyrics is that I have a rather lousy singing voice. And, while I can belt out a great tune on the piano, it is still not good enough to play in public. So, why did God give me this incredible love of music, when it's painfully obvious that one of my greatest 'loves' will never be used for the 'greater good'? I don't have any definitive answer to that, other than if I had been good at singing or playing the piano, then perhaps that would have distracted me from God's ultimate plan for my life.

What I do know is that my ability to memorise hundreds of song lyrics shows me that my brain has a tremendous capacity to store and recall information, and playing the piano is the only way I have found to truly relax. Who knows what God may have in store for my future – there may be a place for music within my purpose that is as yet unknown. Until that time, I am content to enjoy this part of my life privately rather than publicly.

Is it wrong, then, to spend my precious time appreciating music, or playing the piano? Not at all! These things may never become part of my purpose in a tangible way, but they make up the intricate fusion of what makes me me, and I wouldn't be the complete 'me' without all these facets.

Do you have a great love, but can't yet see how it fits into God's plan? Perhaps He intends for you to develop that part of your life further, or have more life experience behind you before he uses your love in a purpose-focused way. Maybe He is saying more of a "not yet" than a "no".

BEWARE CERTAIN LOVES

The Bible warns us that there are some things we love that can get us into trouble. Three of the most notable are found in 2 Timothy 3:1–5 (NKJV): money, ourselves and pleasures.

"But know this, that in the last days perilous times will come: For men will be lovers of themselves, lovers of money, boasters, proud, blasphemers, disobedient to parents, unthankful, unholy, unloving, unforgiving, slanderers, without self-control, brutal, despisers of good, traitors, headstrong, haughty, lovers of pleasure rather than lovers of God, having a form of godliness but denying its power. And from such people turn away!"

And you may be familiar with this well-known verse from 1 Timothy 6:10 (NKJV): *"For the love of money is a root of all kinds of evil, for which some have strayed from the faith in their greediness, and pierced themselves through with many sorrows."*

We live in a me-first society. Everything seems to revolve around 'self' – accumulating possessions and wealth, or doing what feels good or feels right at the expense of doing what is good and godly.

1 Corinthians 13 is known as the 'love chapter'. The Apostle Paul confirms in verse 13 (NIV) that *"…now these three remain: faith, hope and love. But the greatest of these is love."* Love is an emotion given to us directly from God, and He esteems it higher even than faith or hope. The onus is on us to make sure that we keep our love (and our loves) in check.

Be brutally honest when you fill in the list of things you love, and especially consider the question *"what things, people or activities do you spend the most time, money or attention on?"* This honesty can illuminate areas of your life that may need some adjustment before you can walk boldly in your God-given purpose. You can put your list before God and ask Him to show you anything that you may need to deal with and ask Him to help you.

THE GREATEST COMMANDMENT

We cannot close out a section on 'your loves' without looking at what the Bible refers to as 'the greatest commandment'. Jesus Christ himself taught us this important lesson in Mark 12:28–31 (NIV):

"One of the teachers of the law came and heard them debating. Noticing that Jesus had given them a good answer, he asked him, "Of all the commandments, which is the most important?"

"The most important one," answered Jesus, "is this: 'Hear, O Israel: The Lord our God, the Lord is one. Love the Lord your God with all your heart and with all your soul and with all your mind and with all your strength.' The second is this: 'Love your neighbour as yourself.' There is no commandment greater than these."

If you are in any doubt as to where to direct the love that is within you and where your priorities should lie, then these verses should help.

Purpose Discovery Wheel

STEP 6

Your bankable skills

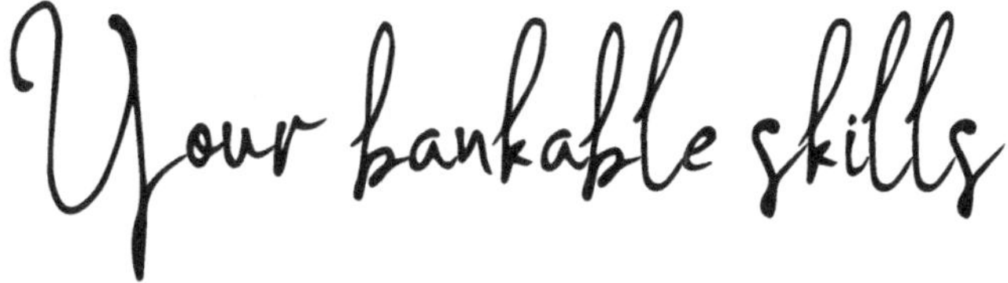

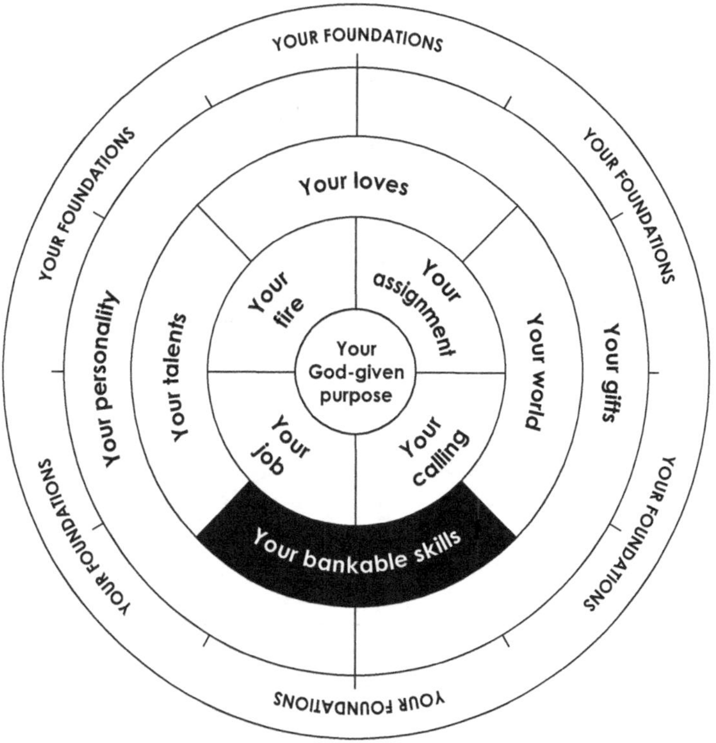

DEFINITION OF 'BANKABLE SKILLS'

- Things you can do that are likely to make money or to produce financial success.
- Things you can be paid for (e.g. in a job or by creating your own business).
- Your bankable skills will develop with time and experience.

Question

What are your top 3–5 bankable skills?

To help you answer this question, consider the following:

- What have people paid you to do in the past?
- What could people pay you to do in the future?
- What skills could you monetise?
- What gaps could you fill in the market?

____

____

____

____

____

____

____

____

____

Early civilisations lived off the land and bartered for goods they required. These days we live in a society with heavily-regulated monetary systems. To buy what we need we have to have some method of earning a living, hence the need for 'bankable skills'. One thing is for sure: we were never meant to sit idle. God designed us to work right from the first human that He created – Adam: "*Then the Lord God took the man [Adam] and put him into the garden of Eden to cultivate it and keep it.*" (Genesis 2:15, NASB).

Very few Christians will ever work in 'full-time ministry' where they do not earn a wage per se, but rather live on financial support (either from their church, organisation or through sponsors). The majority of us will end up either working for someone else or ourselves. Therefore, God is interested and invested in your bankable skills and the jobs you will do throughout your life; they will become intertwined with your calling, your assignments and your purpose which we will explore in Steps 10, 11 and 12.

Purpose Discovery Wheel

STEP 7

Your world

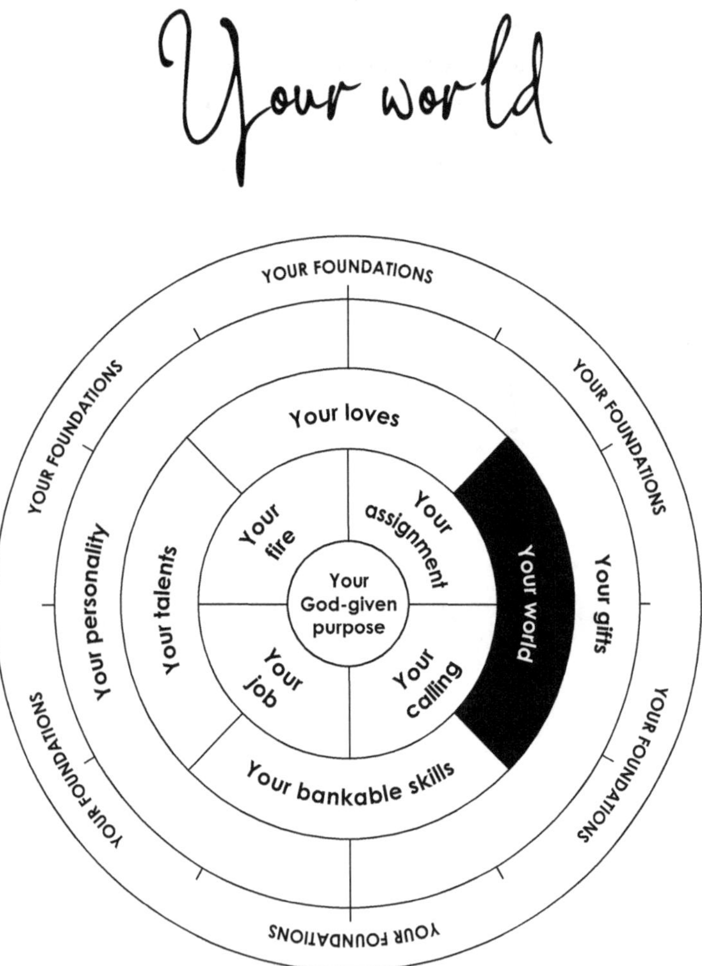

DEFINITION OF 'YOUR WORLD'

- This is 'your' world, not 'the' world. Think about your family, your workplace, the industry you work in; your church, community, society or country.
- The issues affecting your world will change over time.
- Identifying what is important to your world helps you to identify the WHERE question: where will you outwork your purpose?

What does your world need?

To help you answer this question, consider the following:

- What do you have a 'heart for'?
- What group of people do you feel needs help the most?
- What issues or causes do you feel most strongly about?
- What would your world look like if it were operating perfectly according to you?
- What are the things that are most important to you?
- What news items make you mad?
- What might you watch on TV that will make you cry?
- What things do you see around you that could be improved?

After you have considered these questions, what are your top three to five answers? Do you see any themes or patterns running through your list? Is there a particular need that keeps surfacing in your mind?

Put your list into priority order with what you feel is the most important answer at the top.

I like the term that Christians often use when they say they have a 'heart for' something, such as "I have a heart for the lost"…or "for solo mothers"…or "for young people", etc. It indicates a level of interest, empathy and compassion that goes far deeper than the mind (an intellectual response), or the body (a physical response), and cuts through to your spirit or your 'heart'.

Starting to pinpoint the areas you feel most strongly about, in the world around you, can be a good indicator of the place where you will outwork some or all of your God-given assignments.

Though not directly connected on the *Purpose Discovery Wheel*, 'your world' and 'your fire' are closely aligned. Identifying things that your world needs can often stir up the fire in your belly, so once you've worked through Step 8 (your 'fire'), come back here to Step 7 (your world) to see if you missed anything off this list. Conversely, when you look at the question for Step 8, take a peek back here to see if this list helps you to figure out the things that can be a driving force and motivation in your life.

Purpose Discovery Wheel

STEP 8

Your 'fire'

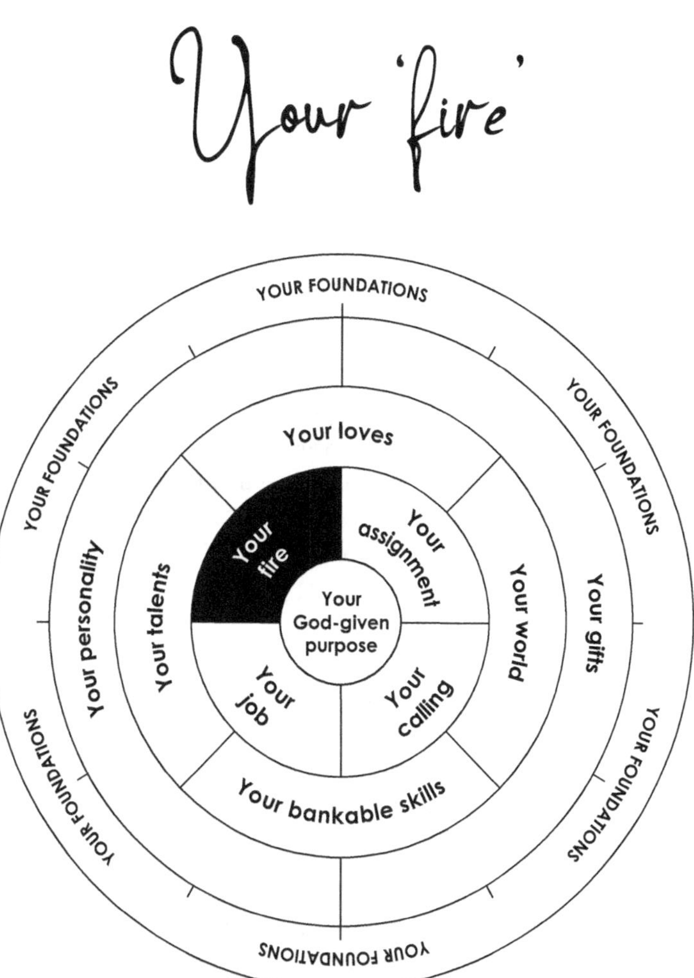

DEFINITION OF 'YOUR FIRE'

- Your 'fire' can be known by several other pretty awesome words, such as passion, desire, fervour, zeal, earnestness, avidness, eagerness, keenness, enthusiasm, excitement, animation, vigour, energy, heat, spirit, zest, appetite, hunger, urgency, dedication, devoutness.
- 'Fire' is the driving force that challenges you, intrigues you, and motivates you to do amazing things.
- Your 'fire' doesn't have to be something you are good at doing.
- Your 'fire' may or may not change over time.

PURPOSE DISCOVERY WHEEL CROSSOVER

Take a look at the wheel, and you will notice that 'your fire' sits between 'your loves' and 'your talents'. It's possible that the thing (or things) that fire you up will be a crossover of what you love in life and your skills and abilities. However, it's also important to remember that 'fire' is a different and more propelling feeling than love or something you happen to be good at doing.

What sets the core of your being on fire?
To help you answer this question, consider the following:

- What would your friends say you were really interested in or passionate about?
- What topic of conversation will keep you up talking until late at night or cause you to lose track of time?
- What would you most like to do for others?
- When do you feel 'in the zone' or 'in the flow'?
- What brings the most satisfaction and meaning to your life?
- What topics inspire you to get actively involved or engaged?
- What energises you?
- What are you willing to make sacrifices for?

- What bothers you or makes you angry?
- What brings a tear to your eye or well-up with emotion?
- What gives you a goose-bump reaction?
- What are your most 'authentic' moments?

After you have considered these questions, what are your top three to five answers?

____

____

____

____

____

____

____

____

Step 8 in our *Purpose Discovery Wheel* is not for the couch-sitter or bystander. This step is all about **action**, **movement** and **intensity** (even if, right now, the action is all in your mind and heart and hasn't yet stepped outside your front door).

'Fire' (passion, and drive) is God-given. It's His way of giving us the motivation to execute our purpose.

The journey of life is never smooth – it's more like a roller coaster, where you will have times of low-lows, high-highs and the occasional season of smooth sailing in between. Having a strong 'fire' within you is the fuel that you need when the low-lows occur (and that's a 'when', not an 'if'). Without a strong sense of motivation, you will be far more likely to give up on your assignment when times get tough.

DESIRE

"Trust in the Lord and do good; dwell in the land and enjoy safe pasture. Take delight in the Lord, and He will give you the desires of your heart. Commit your way to the Lord; trust in Him, and He will do this: He will make your righteous reward shine like the dawn, your vindication like the noonday sun." (Psalm 37:3–6, NIV)

'Desire' is a powerful word. Used in this context, desire is not a feeling driven by the mind or the body, it's driven by the heart and is far stronger than your 'like' for something, or even your 'love' for something.

The word 'desire' can also be described as 'hunger' or 'thirst'. Hunger and thirst are natural expressions of the basic human need for food and water. One of the clear indicators that something is physically wrong is when we lose our appetite. It is the same spiritually. If you have no spiritual desire (for God or for what God is doing within you) then you will feel no drive or 'fire', and that is a warning sign that you need to address; but how do you do that?

As Psalm 37:4 (above) tells us, IF we take delight in the Lord (through praise and thanksgiving), commit our way to Him, and trust in Him, THEN He will give us the desires of our heart. Notice that there are three conditions to His promise. If we do all three, then he will unlock the desire that He has already placed within us. If you are wondering why you may not be able to identify a 'fire' burning within you, then go back and look at the checklist: thanksgiving, committing your ways, and trusting in Him; those are significant conditions to his promise, so you may need to do some work on one or more of these areas.

Once you're able to identify your purpose, then your 'fire' will be the key to keeping you motivated and propelling you forward.

STEP 9

Your job

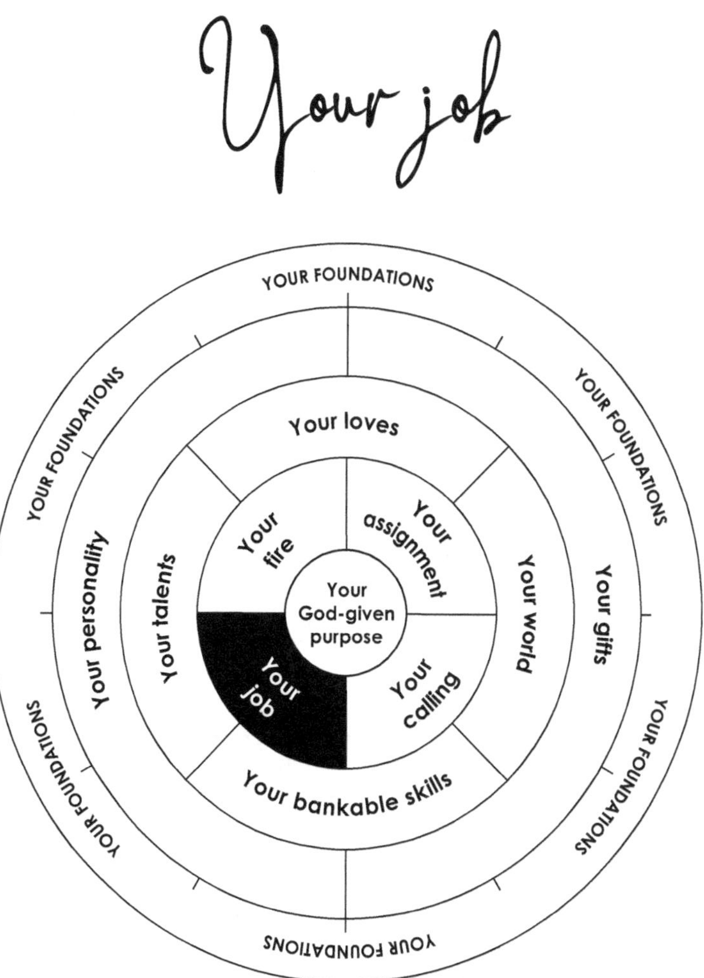

DEFINITION OF 'JOB'

- Your job is a paid occupation or 'profession' that requires some form of study or training.
- You may or may not feel drawn to this.
- Your job will likely change over time.

PURPOSE DISCOVERY WHEEL CROSSOVER

Take a look at the wheel, and you will notice that 'your job' sits between 'your talents' and 'your bankable skills'. It's highly likely that any job you hold (previous, current and future) will be a crossover of what you do well and what you can earn money for.

Question 1

What job(s) have you held over the years?

____

____

____

____

____

____

____

____

Most of the stories we read in the Bible centre on the time of that person's ministry or the impact that they had in history. Often very little is known about the years leading up to their notable works or biblical mention.

Jesus Christ is one of those people of whom little is known about for the first 30 years of his life. What we do know is that he lived in the town of Nazareth in the northern region of Israel. His earthly father, Joseph, was a carpenter (Matthew 13:55) and Jesus followed in his footsteps learning the trade (Mark 6:3).

Here are some other biblical figures and the professions that they held either before or during their time of moving in their God-given purpose.

- **Doctor**. Luke (Colossians 4:14).
- **Fisherman**. Simon Peter, James, John, Andrew and Zebedee (Matthew 4:18, 21).
- **Governor**. Joseph (Genesis 42:6); Daniel (Daniel 6:2), Pilate (Matthew 27:2).
- **Landowner**. Boaz (Ruth 2:3).
- **King**. David (2 Samuel 2), Saul (1 Samuel 9), Herod (Matthew 2:1).
- **Priest**. Melchizedek (Genesis 14:18), Jethro (Exodus 3:1), Aaron (Exodus 28:1).
- **Queen**. Esther (Esther 2:17).
- **Shepherd**. David (1 Samuel 16:8), Moses (Exodus 3:1).
- **Silversmith**. Demetrius (Acts 19:24).
- **Tax collector**. Matthew (Matthew 9:9).
- **Tent maker**. Paul, Aquila and Priscilla (Acts 18:1-3).
- **Wine maker**. Noah (Genesis 9:20).

"SO, WHAT DO YOU DO FOR A LIVING?"

Ahh…one of the all-time favourite question-starters in the world of small talk. When you meet someone new, a question regarding your job is inevitably one of the first things that you'll be asked. It is as if by receiving your answer that the questioner will be able to judge the type of person you are, where you 'fit' into society and whether or not you are someone they wish to continue associating with. The good news is that what other people think about your job choice pales by comparison to knowing that you are working in the right place at the right time for the right reasons.

Your job or profession is what you do to pay your bills and put food on the table; it does not define who you are or God's purpose for your life. However, given that you will likely spend at least $^1/_3$ of each day doing job-related activities, it's important that the work you do fits into God's overall purpose for your life. It's also important that you derive some measure of satisfaction and remuneration for the time you invest – as it says in 1 Timothy 5:18 (NIV), "*The worker deserves his wages.*" And, if you find yourself in a job that you do not enjoy, then you can lean on this verse until you are able to move into a more suitable role: "*Whatever your hand finds to do, do it with all your might.*" (Ecclesiastes 9:10)

The ideal is to find yourself in a job or career where you can use the abilities and gifts that God has placed within you. If you can combine your talents, gifts and bankable skills with something that you love to do, then you will start to live a more rounded, happier life.

WHY YOUR JOB IS IMPORTANT

Some people know – from a very young age – precisely what they want to do when they grow up. Others may stumble from one job or career path to another. It so happened that I started as a bit of a stumbler myself.

As a teenager, my dream was to become a zoo keeper. The kicker was that our zoo didn't hire junior keepers until they were at least 21 years old, and so that meant I had a four-year gap to fill.

So, I started out doing a tertiary science course until I realised that learning science and biology was not for me (bye-bye zoo keeping). From that point, my career has bounced along as follows: photolithography; graphic design; agency account management; recruitment, and human resources. Whilst these jobs were all different, I've always remained within the creative communications and digital industries.

My work journey is a reflection of how my creative interests and my talents in design and administration have been utilised to earn a living and pay the bills. However, it has only been within the last few years that I've seen my job dovetail with my calling, assignments and purpose. I know, now, that being in the business world is part of my calling, and God has been leading me along this winding job route my whole adult life.

Through each of my jobs, I have accumulated many of the life experiences, teachable moments, people interactions, conversations, relationships, highs and lows that have combined to help me help others (both personally and professionally).

I often joke that I had to kiss a few job-frogs before I found my prince, but at the same time, I know that even job-frogs contain valuable lessons, knowledge and skill-developing moments. It's up to us to squeeze all the juicy goodness out of each workplace we are in, and take every opportunity we can to pour some of that goodness back into the people we work with.

You never know, God may reveal that His purpose for you has something directly to do with your job or your colleagues. If not, at the very minimum, you are God's ambassador wherever He places you, so it's important to keep your eyes and heart open and your integrity and reputation intact.

FOR THOSE JUST STARTING OUT...

"I told the careers advisor at school that I wanted to run away with the circus. They said it would never happen, but that's exactly what I did! I ended up performing overseas in a touring circus, all around Asia. It

was super, super cool." (Skye Haddy, ex-gymnast, ex-cheerleader and Australia Ninja Warrior competitor, 2020)

The following is a brief, yet powerful excerpt from actor Chadwick Boseman's 2018 commencement speech at his alma mater, Howard University (USA). Boseman (who passed away in September 2020) encourages the students to tap into their purpose and trust that God will make a way for them as they move forward in their careers.

"*God says, in Jeremiah, "I know the plans I have for you, plans to prosper you and not to harm you; plans to give you hope and a future.*"

"*Sometimes you need to feel the pain and sting of defeat to activate the real passion and purpose that God predestined inside of you.*

"*Graduating class, here me well on this day. This day when you have reached the hilltop, and you are deciding on next jobs, and next steps, careers, further education – you would rather find purpose than a job or career. Purpose crosses disciplines. Purpose is an essential element of you. It is the reason you are on the planet at this particular time in history. Your very existence is wrapped up in the things you are here to fulfil.*

"*Whatever you choose for a career path, remember the struggles along the way are only meant to shape you for your purpose.*

"*When God has something for you, it doesn't matter who stands against it. God will move someone who is holding you back, away from a door, and put someone there who will open it for you if it's meant for you.*

"*I don't know what your future is, but if you are willing to take the harder way; the more complicated one; the one with more failures at first than successes; the one that has ultimately proven to have more meaning, more victory, more glory, then you will not regret it.*"

WHAT ABOUT A SIDE HUSTLE?

Have you ever heard the phrase 'side hustle'? It means something that you do on the sideline (and separate from your primary job) that can earn you money, or something that you do on the side gratis (without charge; free).

Side hustles can be undertakings that people feel passionate about, rather than a typical 'day job' worked to make ends meet. Often side hustles will build to the point where you can earn enough money to give up your day-job, and focus on what you genuinely love doing.

A side hustle may simply be a way of moving from one job to another, but it can also be a gateway to outworking your calling and purpose.

Side hustles usually require you to find time – outside of your normal working hours – to concentrate on developing your new endeavour. I've always held firmly to the belief that if you want to do something strongly enough, you will find time for it.

My first published book was the size of four university theses (around 130,000 words). During the time of writing, I held a 40-hour-per-week job, plus I spent up to two hours per day in traffic getting to and from work. That didn't leave much time in any 24 hours to create the behemoth of a book, but I did it, and it only took me two years!

Where did I 'find the time' to write this tome? I prioritised that book over many other things. I sacrificed time with friends, family, going out, socialising or watching TV. I was even proof-reading my book while lying on a beach in Fiji on 'holiday'. I'm not saying that all of my sacrifices were wise, but they were the choices that I made at the time. It's only through having a 'fire' and a sense of purpose (or some other exceptionally strong motivation) that can drive a side hustle or assignment along in that manner.

Be careful and prayerful. While a side-hustle (or significant project) may seem like a good idea, you have to know that the time, money and other resources that you invest will be worth it in God's currency, not just man's; and that your effort will not become a distraction from your purpose and path.

SHOULD I GIVE UP MY JOB?

Does God want you to start a side hustle, reduce your hours or even give up your job so you can put more time and effort into your calling or assignment? I wish I could advise you, but you'll need to ask God directly on that one. It could be that your day job is just where God needs you to be right now and that the people in your workplace (or the wider industry that you work in) are exactly the people that God wants to reach through you. Sometimes you have to look past the job itself and the tasks you perform and ask the "why here, why now, Lord?" question.

If you wake up each morning with a sinking sensation in the pit of your stomach and the feeling that you couldn't possibly last another day in your job, then it's probably not the right place for you. God didn't intend for you to be in a job that you hate or where you feel miserable or physically sick, so that's a good indicator that you are not in the place you should be, or that the time has come to move on.

"Whatever you do, work heartily, as for the Lord and not for men, knowing that from the Lord you will receive the inheritance as your reward. You are serving the Lord Christ." (Colossians 3:23-24, NASB)

Question 2

Do you think you are in the job where God wants you right now?
Yes / No

If you answered "yes", great! If you answered "no", then what action steps could you take to change your work situation?

- Hint: Action step #1 = pray for wisdom and direction!

-

-

-

Purpose Discovery Wheel

STEP 10

Your calling

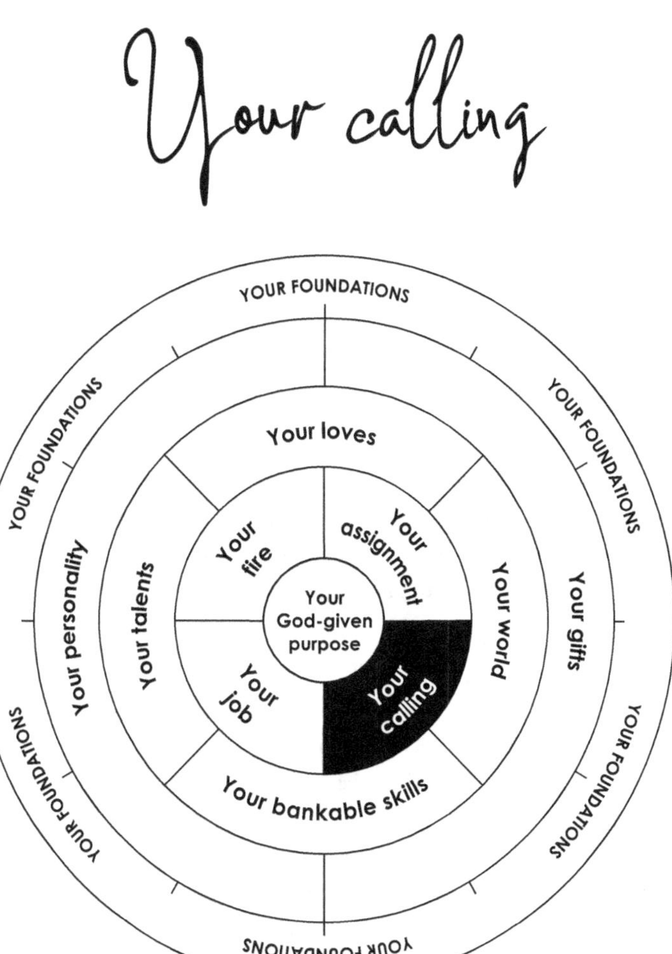

DEFINITION OF 'CALLING'

- Your calling can also be thought of as a meaningful or satisfying 'vocation', 'summons' or 'pursuit'.
- It may be a profession or occupation (or voluntary role) that you feel strongly drawn to (as opposed to a job that you do simply to earn money).
- This could be work that is paid or unpaid.
- It may or may not be related to your job or career.
- You may or may not have received training for this type of work.
- It may change over time.
- Your calling helps to answer a WHAT question: what role will you play within your overall God-given purpose?

PURPOSE DISCOVERY WHEEL CROSSOVER

Take a look at the wheel, and you will notice that 'your calling' sits between 'your bankable skills' and 'your world'. Your calling could be a crossover of what you can earn money for and the issues or causes that you feel most strongly about – while remembering the caveat, that your calling may be a paid or unpaid pursuit.

Examples of a job vs a calling:
- Jesus Christ was a carpenter for a job, but His calling was as a Rabbi (teacher) of God's Word.
- Moses was firstly a prince of Egypt, then a shepherd, but his calling was to courageously lead the Israelites out of Egypt and into the Promised Land.
- I have held a few different jobs, including graphic designer, tertiary design teacher, and agency account director, but my calling is to equip, encourage and inspire individuals and businesses; to help them grow personally, professionally and spiritually.

Question

What can you identify as your calling or vocation?
You may list more than one thing, especially if you feel that your calling is still unclear.

Identifying your calling is not easy for everyone, especially if you are young or in the early stages of your walk with God. The two steps in the *Purpose Discovery Wheel* that usually stump people and which can elicit a blank-face response are 'your calling' and 'your assignment', and that's totally OK.

For some people, like Mother Theresa (whom we read about earlier on) her calling to be a nun was crystal clear from 18 years old, but she would be an exception to the norm. For most of us, our calling develops over time, and after we let God mould and shape us into a vessel that is fit for the purpose He intends for our lives.

As you think on this some more, pray for the Holy Spirit to give you wisdom and clarity. As you gain more practical life experience, and as you pivot according to His plan, your calling will come into focus.

For some people, their day job and their calling will be similar. Take, for example, my husband, Simon. Simon spent a good deal of his working life as a primary school teacher. We also know that Simon has been given the gift of teaching, which is also part of his calling – to study and impart God's Word to equip the Body of Christ (the church).

You may find that you know your broad-brush calling (such as preaching or ministering to the sick). God will take those initial brush strokes, and start to fill in the detail. Your masterpiece will take shape once you layer in your assignment (see Step 11), and begin to see how God will practically outwork your calling. For example, your calling might be 'to help the poor and needy', and your assignment might be 'to work with orphans in Africa'.

STEP 11

Your assignment

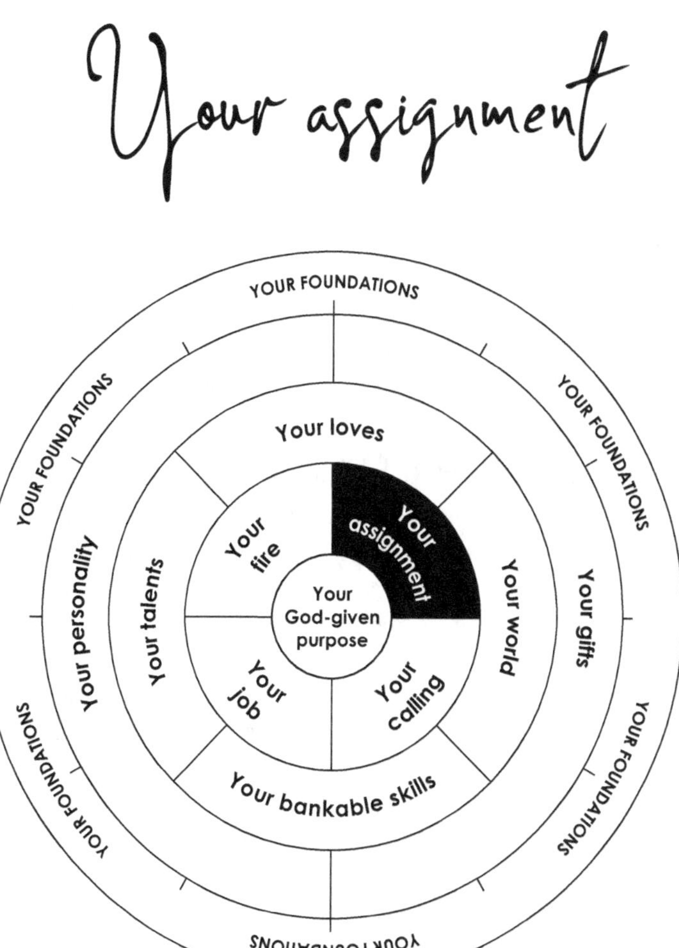

DEFINITION OF 'ASSIGNMENT'

- You can also think of your 'assignment' as your 'mission' or 'contribution'.
- What is an important contribution that you can make to your family, church, workplace, industry, society, country or planet?
- What do you feel that you need to be doing?
- Your assignment could be personal or professional.
- It may change over time.
- God will usually give you a series of assignments throughout your life.
- Your assignment refers to an ACTION – something you already do, or want to do, or will do in the future. It helps to answer the WHERE and HOW questions: where will you outwork your purpose? OR, how will you outwork your purpose?

PURPOSE DISCOVERY WHEEL CROSSOVER

Take a look at the wheel, and you will notice that 'your assignment' sits between 'your loves' and 'your world'. It's highly likely that your assignment(s) will be a crossover of the things you love in life and the issues or causes that you feel most strongly about.

The caveat here is that not all of God's assignments will be enjoyable (or based on things you love to do). Remember the Biblical account of Jonah? In Jonah 1:1–3 (NIV) it reads *"The word of the Lord came to Jonah son of Amittai: "Go to the great city of Nineveh and preach against it because its wickedness has come up before me." But Jonah ran away from the Lord and headed for Tarshish. He went down to Joppa, where he found a ship bound for that port. After paying the fare, he went aboard and sailed for Tarshish to flee from the Lord."*

And we all know what happened then; he ended up in the belly of a great fish for three days! When the fish finally vomited Jonah onto dry land, Jonah ended up going to Nineveh as God had originally requested. Though not always enjoyable, God has a reason for selecting our assignments. Unless you want to end up in the belly of a fish, it's usually easier to just say "yes, Lord, and Amen"!

Question

What can you identify as your divine assignment?
You may list more than one thing, especially if you feel that your assignment is still unclear.

____

____

____

____

____

____

As a child of God, you don't decide your assignment, you discover it. However, don't be disheartened if you cannot identify your God-given assignment, as this knowledge will come in time.

For me, I was 40 years old before I felt that I had a specific job that God wanted me to do, and 40 years is a long time to wait (just ask Moses!). Before that time, I was meandering through my Christian walk – always occupied, but never feeling intentional or fulfilled.

One reason for this aimlessness was that I did not realise that I could outwork my assignment outside of the church. I grew up believing that all gifts were designed for use within the church; therefore, my assignment had to exist within the church as well. No wonder I felt like I didn't 'fit' into any church team or ministry.

International speaker, author and pastor, Johnny Enlow, says that his mandate is to challenge and equip the church to influence all areas of society with the supernatural love and power of God.

In his book '*The Seven Mountain Prophecy*', Enlow writes about seven primary spheres of society – media, education, government, economy, arts and entertainment, family and religion. He believes that each Christian will have an assignment primarily to one of these seven areas and that our mission is to bring the kingdom of God to that area.

He goes on to say that only 3% of Christians will have an assignment to the sphere of 'religion' (a.k.a. the church, where we typically understand a Christian's 'ministry' focus to be). That means that 97% of us will have our primary assignment to one of the seven mountains of society that is NOT the church mountain, and not in traditional ministry.

Let's take a minute to look at the calling and assignment given to William Wilberforce (1759 – 1833), a Christian politician, philanthropist, and leader of the movement to abolish the slave trade in England. Lance Wallnau references Enlow's Seven Mountains in the following passage:

"Transformation happens in a city or community, just like conversion happens – through a sustained pattern of public persuasion." I got those [words] from William Wilberforce, who eradicated slavery in Great Britain without ever having to fire a bullet.

"How did they eliminate slavery in England and we [in the USA] had to have a civil war? Wilberforce, as a Christian, was in government, and he worked with media and arts and business and education, and he had strong apostolic pastors at his table.

"They commiserated as a fellowship at a business man's estate called Clapham. Progressively, over the course of his life, they launched initiatives, books, productions, discussions and legislation that pinpricked the conscience of Great Britain until it couldn't stand its own hypocrisy any

longer and it had to change its values.

"He created what we call a 'reformation'. Understand the difference between 'reformation' and 'revival' (because we're all revival junkies). Revival is packed-out houses, with phenomenon and glory clouds, signs, wonders and a lot of media buzz – like Billy Graham at Madison Square Garden.

"Reformation is the ugly step-sister of revival. Reformation nobody really wants because reformation isn't personal; reformation is institutional. It goes into those structures [referring to the Seven Mountains] *and changes the way they think. So when you go into business, when you go into academia, and when you go even (as Luther found out) into the religious mountain, if it doesn't respond to what God's doing it will actually get into a fight with you.*

"Reformation is institutional transformation. What Wilberforce did was he worked off Wesley and Whitfield and the Methodists and the move of God and said we've got to use this juice in order to change the way people think – a sustained pattern of public persuasion. They progressively eroded and 'termited' the Devil down until slavery was outlawed.

"On his deathbed, he got to see it. His whole life was dedicated to it. The nation had actually recovered its Christian values. It can be done. But for it to be done, it requires leaders to work together for the purpose of transforming the narrative that is dominating the nation right now."

Wilberforce's job, calling and assignments were all within the 'mountain' of government, and he rose through the ranks of the British parliamentary system until he was in a position of significant influence.

His most notable assignment – to abolish the British slave trade – took 46 long years to come to pass! Wilberforce died just three days after hearing that the passage of the Slavery Abolition Act (1833) through Parliament was assured – a great testament to the idea that God will not take us from this earth until His assignment for us is complete.

Not only was Wilberforce a dedicated abolitionist, he used his position within the British government to champion causes and campaigns such as the Society for the Suppression of Vice, British missionary work in India, the creation of a free colony in Sierra Leone, the foundation of the Church Mission Society, and the Society for the Prevention of Cruelty to Animals. His underlying conservatism led him to support politically and socially controversial legislation. Still, he remained steadfast to the calling and assignments that God had given to him despite opposition.

I see – very clearly now – that my assignments have been in the two mountains of 'economy' and 'arts and entertainment'. When I look back on my life, I've always been involved in both business and the arts in some way, whether that was influencing businesses, running my own businesses, fine art, graphic design, or writing. It's exciting to see how God causes things to come together over time, just as they were meant to do.

I wonder if I had understood about gifts and assignments, earlier on, how different my life might have been; or was God deliberately restraining and training me during those first 40 years? I probably won't know the answer to that question this side of Heaven, but I'm glad I know better now so that I might maximise the time I have left on this earth.

One thing is for sure, if God gives you an assignment then He will also give you the wisdom, strength, endurance, and confidence to conquer your particular mountain; and He will be right there with you because He's already promised: "*I will never leave you nor forsake you.*" (Hebrews 13:5, ESV).

To go on an assignment for God, He can work with you no matter your background. You don't have to prove any prior success or high achievement, and you certainly don't have to hold any credentials. When you have God in you and with you, all He needs is that you accept His will and His plan for your life and say "OK, let's do this…together!"

STEP 12

Your God-given purpose

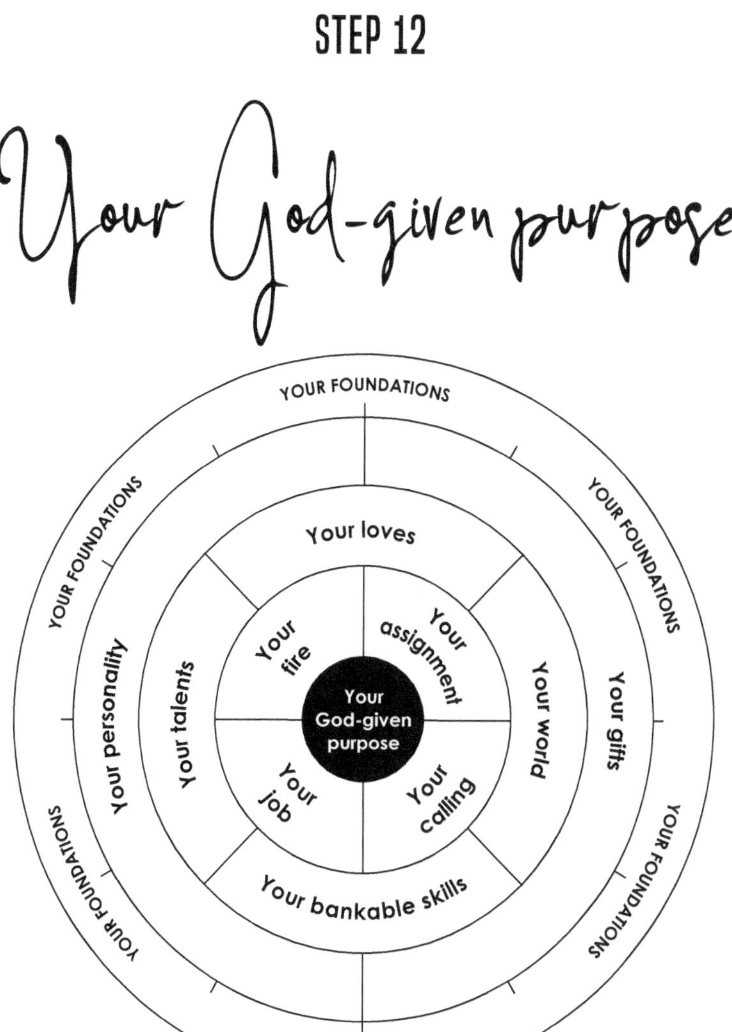

DEFINITION OF 'GOD-GIVEN PURPOSE'

- Your raison d'être (your reason for being).
- Why you get up in the morning.
- What brings you fulfilment, satisfaction and a sense of meaning to life.
- The focus could be personal or professional.

Question 1a

What is your God-given purpose?
To help you answer this question, it's time to review what you wrote for Steps 3 to 11. Choose the answers that you would rank #1, #2 and #3 on each list and write them below.

Step 3: Your gifts

____

____

____

____

Step 4: Your talents

____

____

____

____

Step 5: Your loves

____

____

____

Step 6: Your bankable skills

____

____

____

Step 7: Your world

____

____

____

Step 8: Your 'fire'

____

____

____

Step 9: Your job

____

____

____

Step 10: Your calling

____

____

____

Step 11: Your assignment

____

____

____

- Can you see your story start to unfold when you combine Steps 3 to 11?
- Can you see strong themes emerging or double-ups?
- Can you see how God has been drawing the seemingly different facets of your life together into one amazing picture?
- Can you see your gifts running through any of the other Steps?

As an example, here are my results so you can see how I wrote my final 'purpose-narrative':

Step 3: Your gifts

encouragement

teaching

administration

Step 4: Your talents

organisation

design/creativity/art/writing

conveying information/advising

Step 5: Your loves

encouraging others

teaching/training

writing/words

Step 6: Your bankable skills

a toolbox of technical skills

business/creative comms experience

client service/recruitment/HR

Step 7: Your world

training and equipping for growth

supporting businesses

wise leadership

Step 8: Your 'fire'

encouraging others

helping individuals reach their personal and professional potential

helping businesses grow

Step 9: Your job

Graphic Designer

Agency Account Director

Head of People & Culture

Step 10: Your calling

trainer/advisor/mentor/facilitator

imparting knowledge

helping individuals reach their personal and professional potential

Step 11: Your assignment

To spread the Word through writing

To encourage others and build them up

THEMES THAT FLOWED THROUGH MY ANSWERS:

Teaching/training and encouraging others (note: both of these are also my gifts); a business focus; writing; building people up personally, spiritually and professionally.

MY 'PURPOSE-NARRATIVE' (MY GOD-GIVEN PURPOSE):

1   To encourage, equip and inspire people and businesses.
2   To help individuals reach their full personal, spiritual and professional potential.

I will achieve this through…writing, teaching and using my accumulated skills, experience and technical knowledge to foster growth and spread the Word.

Question 1b

What is your purpose-narrative (your God-given purpose)?

____

____

____

____

____

____

____

____

____

____

____

____

____

What is your purpose-narrative (your God-given purpose)?

Question 1c

How will you achieve your purpose?

Please refer to my purpose-narrative on the previous page as an example

- What do you think of your results? Do they help to give you a broad picture of how God is working in your life?
- Did you get a sense of excitement to see how the various facets of your life are intertwined?
- Are you where you want to be?
- Are there any Steps in the *Purpose Discovery Wheel* that are not yet clear to you? Remember that this is OK and normal – God will reveal the fullness of His plans for you in His time.

Where to from here?

USING YOUR GOD-GIVEN PURPOSE AS A FILTER

Are you still struggling to pinpoint your purpose, or wondering how it can practically outwork in your life? The reality is that you may not experience a bolt of lightning or total clarity of purpose or direction. So what can you do? You can pull all of your introspection together and use it as a filter (or lens) through which you can make future decisions.

For example, life may present you with a new opportunity, and that's the perfect time to filter your decision through your *Purpose Discovery Wheel* results. Does the opportunity fit in with your 'fire', calling, assignment, etc.? If the opportunity does not fit that formula, then it may be better not to do it. Ideally, everything you do should be an expression of your purpose. If the opportunity doesn't align with your purpose, then you have to question whether it is going to be a wise investment of your time and resources, or whether it will be a distraction from what God wants you to do. Knowing your purpose will help to simplify your life.

DO YOU HAVE TO CHANGE?

To begin with, to know your purpose, you have to know God – the author and giver of the purpose for your life. If you do not currently have a relationship with God, through Jesus Christ and what He did for you on the cross, then please refer back to the first chapter of *Pur-*

pose Made "Why are we here?". If you need to, now is the time to make that big step-change, and I promise that you will never regret it!

For those of us who already have a relationship with God, then most of the personal and spiritual development that we experience in life happens by degrees. Why don't you talk with God about your results? Firstly ask Him if the results are accurate and talk with Him about areas that are not so clear to you at this point.

You can then ask God to illuminate areas of your life that may need an adjustment. Sometimes those adjustments will be tweaks; at other times they will need a 180-degree overhaul. Ask Him for wisdom to know what to do and when to do it, and He will tell you.

Remember that God will not make you do what you don't want to do. Good and lasting change can only happen with a heart that is willing.

WHAT IF YOUR PURPOSE ISN'T CLEAR?

There is a chance that you may have completed Step 12 and are still left wondering what your God-given purpose is. That's totally normal, especially if you are young in years or early in your Christian walk.

My first piece of advice is to put your results, thoughts and petitions before God and ask Him to give you a revelation of His plan for your life.

Ask him to show you if any blockages are preventing you from understanding or progressing in His will for your life, and then ask Him to show you how to deal with those barriers.

Hopefully, you will have gleaned enough information, from the *Purpose Discovery Wheel* to at least give you some semblance of what the elements of your purpose look like. You can start by living in what you do know of your purpose (or calling, or assignments, etc.) little by little, every day. Listen to the feedback and counsel you receive from others, and be aware of the fruit that you are producing, and things will become more apparent over time.

While you are waiting for God to reveal His plans (in His time), you can at least start to move in God's purpose, which is to establish His kingdom on the earth (as we discussed in the 'Why are we here?' chapter of this book). Ultimately, your individual purpose will dovetail into God's purpose for mankind in some way.

Here is an encouraging quote from Kat Kerr, from her book '*Revealing Heaven*': "*We must use the gifts He gave us while on Earth. If you do not know what your destiny is, then love God and others as yourself, and He will make sure you do not miss your destiny.*"

Keep your eyes and heart looking heavenward, and God will come through for you.

YOUR PURPOSE IN THE DAY-TO-DAY

In Psalm 90:12 (ESV), the Psalmist is asking God to "*Teach us to number our days, that we may gain a heart of wisdom.*" We are all accountable for the days that God has given to us, and none of us knows how many days we have been allotted. Now that you have some clarity around your God-given purpose, how might that outwork in your everyday life, so you can make the wisest and fullest use of the time you have been given?

WITH YOUR FAMILY AND FRIENDS

Have you ever found that the people who know you the best are often your harshest critics and the hardest to convince? The best way to live out your purpose within your circle of family and friends is by steadfastly doing what you know you are purposed to do, and then others will see the fruit you produce. Words alone can be empty, so you have to walk the talk with integrity, humility, empathy and grace, and – eventually – your actions will have an impact.

Sam Cawthorn, the Founder and CEO of the Speakers Institute, Australia said "*have a clarity of purpose and know your 'why'. If you have this, people will see the conviction in your eyes; they will see your determination.*"

Without knowing your overarching purpose, your endeavours may seem haphazard and confusing to others. Once you know your purpose (and can articulate it), your efforts will begin to make sense. Your friends and family may or may not choose to support you, but at the very least they will start to understand your 'why'.

IN YOUR CHURCH

As we looked at, in **Step 11: Your assignment**, only around 3% of Christians will find that their overarching purpose, and subsequent God-given assignments, lie within the walls of their local church. For the rest of us, our areas of focus will be in other areas of society such as workplaces, industries, communities, schools, retirement villages, government, etc.

However, what God did intend was for our God-given, Jesus-given and Holy Spirit-given gifts (along with our talents and skills) to be used within the church for the equipping and blessing of fellow Christians. It is important, then, that you ensure that you understand what your gifts are (refer to **Step 3: Your gifts**).

Whilst everyone can (and usually does) do tasks within the church (because they need doing), you will find that you'll have a higher level of satisfaction, enthusiasm and dedication to those tasks if you align your service to your area of gifting.

Have a chat with your church leadership or eldership to let them know what your gifts are and see what opportunities open up for you. If there is no opportunity currently available, perhaps you could suggest starting something new.

IN YOUR WORKPLACE OR INDUSTRY

Before going on my own purpose discovery journey, I thought that I went to work just to pay the bills. Having this mindset meant that I was resentful of the disproportionately-high amount of time that I spent at work. I felt that my job took me away from doing things that I wanted to do, and what I felt were 'God-centred' activities. Since working through the *Purpose Made* process, I have changed the way that I look at my job.

As we found out in **Step 6: Your bankable skills**, from the time the first person walked on this earth (Adam), humankind has worked in some capacity, tending the land and hunting or farming animals. Work is not separated from us; work is integral to our life, our spirituality and who we are. It's not a case of achieving a 'work/life balance' – work IS part of life and part of our greater purpose.

With this knowledge, I have now reframed my narrative and the way I think about my job. I know that God's purpose for me can and does outwork in my day-to-day employment. I also know that I have been put on this earth to impact businesses as well as to teach and equip those within the church. Where I once resented my job and the time it consumes, I can now look at my work-based opportunities, and my colleagues, through a purpose-shaped lens. Once upon a time, going to work caused me frustration, now it creates a sense of excitement to uncover the potential in everyday situations and conversations.

But what if you have to take a job out of sheer necessity and desperation, where you feel you are working outside of your talents, skills and training? Be assured that even then God is in the situation. It is often in those times of extreme need that God will use your circumstances for His good.

Think about the people around you and ask God to open up opportunities to bless others – with a timely word, or an action, or a smile. While you may feel that the place you are working is not part of your overall purpose, you may be pleasantly surprised!

IN YOUR WIDER WORLD

In **Step 7: Your world**, you looked at the world around you. You listed the things that tug at your heart, bring a tear to your eye, or stir up a righteous passion within you. You figured out the causes, sectors of society, people groups, charities, and so forth that hold a special place of interest within you.

I hope that by the time you reached Step 12, you could see God's plan for your life, and His plan for your world around you taking shape.

Here is an encouraging word from Greg Crawford, Pastor of City Impact Church (Auckland, New Zealand): "*You have been created on purpose for a purpose. We all have 168 hours in a week, so do the most you can, in those hours, for the sake of the kingdom. [God] needs you to be available to people who He will bring into your world (not my world, your world). God's wired us up for a unique purpose, for the sake of His body and the kingdom. Never say "I'm just a…" or "I'm only a…", not when you've got Christ in you. You ARE a!*"

Indeed, you ARE a VIP – a Very Important Purpose-Led-Person within your world, so how is that going to unfold moving forward? That's a great question to ask God and wait eagerly on His answer. One thing I do know is that the people within your world will be in for a real blessing once your combination of gifts, personality, talents, skills and 'fire' are released!

REMEMBER THAT YOU ARE 100% UNIQUE

Did you know that God has created 7.8 billion DIFFERENT people who are walking around on this planet (take a moment to register that number!)? I don't know about you, but that number blows me away.

Not only are our DNA and fingerprints unique, but so is our purpose. That's over 7.8 billion different purposes (think about that for a moment too).

There exists a finite number of gifts and personality traits. If you combined these finite elements alone, the chances of two people having the same gift and set of personality traits would be infinitesimal.

Then, take those finite elements and combine them with your special mix of talents, loves, bankable skills, 'fire', job, calling, assignment and the world around you, and all of a sudden you are presented with a combination that only you possess. Your resulting, God-given purpose is yours alone and can never, ever be replicated. Isn't God incredible?!

Please take some time to let that thought sink into your heart. Science already tells you that you are physically one-of-a-kind. The Bible tells you that you were thought of BEFORE you were put into your mother's womb and that you are loved beyond measure. Now, I hope you can see how very special you are, that you are here on this earth for a specific reason and that God does not (ever, ever, ever) make mistakes!

Conclusion

Many years ago, I was listening to an interview on the radio. The interviewee had conducted a study to determine what the best emotion in the world was, and the result was surprising.

I would have expected people to say 'love' or 'joy' or 'hope', but the top result was 'relief', and that made me stop and think.

In the context of this book, relief could be what it feels like when you finally get clarity on God's will for your life, and all the years of pent-up frustration start to melt away. Relief could be when you start to strip away wrong or limiting mindsets and begin to move in the freedom that only God can give. Relief could be when you finally see yourself as God has always seen you – strong, amazing, loved and created for a reason.

I hope that you have had moments of 'relief' as you have worked your way through *Purpose Made*. I hope that you can now see that you have been placed here on this earth for a specific and unique reason.

You have a contribution that only you can make and a story that only you can tell, and I hope that you will flourish in that knowledge.

We started this book with song lyrics, so it's only fitting that we finish the same way. You may be familiar with the song '*New Wine*' by Hillsong Worship. Even if you are not, try reading these lyrics as if they are a prayer from you to God.

'NEW WINE'
HILLSONG WORSHIP

In the crushing, in the pressing,
You are making new wine.
In the soil, I now surrender;
You are breaking new ground.

So I yield to You and to Your careful hand.
When I trust You, I don't need to understand.

Make me Your vessel, make me an offering;
Make me whatever You want me to be.
I came here with nothing, but all You have given me;
Jesus, bring new wine out of me.

'Cause where there is new wine there is new power;
There is new freedom, and the kingdom is here.
I lay down my old flames to carry Your new fire today.

©Hillsong Worship
Songwriter: Brooke Ligertwood

I want to express my heartfelt gratitude to you for joining me on this journey of self-discovery and personal growth.

Remember, you are unique – fearfully and wonderfully made by our Creator God who loves you beyond measure. Your life is purposeful, and you have the power to make a positive impact on this world – your world.

I encourage you to take these lessons to heart and apply them to your life. May you walk confidently in the direction of your purpose and live a life of abundance.

If you would like to get in touch, please contact me via the contact form on my website, **www.sarah-ritchie.com**. I would love to hear your story, especially if this book has made a positive impact on your life.

I want to give my specific thanks to the following people who have been generous to share their thoughts and experiences with me. Thanks also to all those people who have encouraged and supported me throughout this process. You are amazing!

Christina Bell	Cheryl Megchelse	Allanah Tatana
Michael Fearne	Zeal Nicholas	Dane Tatana
Gary Flockhart	Grant Ritchie	Cynthia Thomas
Karolyn Flockhart	Madeleine Ritchie	Monica Thomas
Tina Graham	Robin Ritchie	Andy Thomson
Mari Grobler	Simon Ritchie	Warwick Thomson
Shirley Kokich	Andy Robilliard	Simon Todd
Peter Liow	Nick Sedwell	Nancy Tsen
Kat Loizides	Elaine Spearman	Kristina Vickery
Christine Mata	Amanda Stewart	Tracy Willis

In 2011 Andres Zuzunaga created 'The Zuzunaga Venn Diagram of Purpose'. Zuzunaga's original diagram contained nine sections titled 'what you love'; what you are good at'; 'what the world needs'; 'what you can be paid for'; 'passion'; 'mission'; 'vocation'; 'profession' and 'purpose'.

Zuzunaga's diagram was intended to help people find personal structure in a chaotic world, and tried to answer questions like *"what are we here for?"* and *"why were we born?"*

As far as I have been able to tell, Zuzunaga does not hold to the Christian faith, yet I saw the intrinsic merit behind his diagram.

In 2014, Zuzunaga's diagram was merged with the Japanese concept of 'ikigai' (a reason for being) by Marc Winn, who replaced the word at the centre of the diagram ('purpose') with 'ikigai'. A few years later, this altered diagram went viral, and people worldwide believed the diagram to represent ikigai. This supposition is now acknowledged to be incorrect.

Prior to writing this book I used Zuzunaga's diagram to run purpose discovery workshops, layering in my own interpretation over the diagram. These sessions were highly successful, especially when working with people in a non-faith-based manner.

While I knew *The Zuzunaga Venn Diagram of Purpose* to be sound and well-tested, I felt it was missing reference to the one who created our purpose in the first place. Without including God in discussions about purpose, you will still be left with a God-sized hole in your results. This hole can be difficult to fill for someone who does not hold to the Christian faith, and they may never understand why they still feel unfulfilled.

The 12 steps of the *Purpose Discovery Wheel* are based on the nine original sections (slightly re-worded), with the addition of three new sections.

The journey through *Purpose Made*, and the *Purpose Discovery Wheel* shows how powerful discovering your purpose can be once you combine Zuzunaga's original idea with the 'God-factor', and uncover a more eternal perspective for your life.

Bibliography

Abraham, Lauren. "The power of patience." Grand Canyon University. <https://www.gcu.edu/blog/spiritual-life/weekly-devotional-power-patience>Arcadia Farms. "7 reasons to appreciate winter." LocalHarvest.org <https://www.localharvest.org/blog/50346/entry/7_reasons_to_appreciate_winter>

Bernock, Danielle. "Is it true that God will never give us more than we can handle?" Christianity.com <https://www.christianity.com/wiki/bible/god-will-never-give-us-more-than-we-can-handle.html>

Bible Resources. "How old was Timothy when he was ordained by Paul?". Bibleresources.info. <https://bibleresources.info/how-old-was-timothy-when-he-was-ordained-by-paul/>

Bible Study Tools. "Predestination." <https://www.biblestudytools.com/dictionary/predestination/>

Brienes Ph.D., Juliana. "3 ways your beliefs can shape your reality". Psychology Today. <https://www.psychologytoday.com/nz/blog/in-love-and-war/201508/3-ways-your-beliefs-can-shape-your-reality>

Campbell, Roger D. "Three Old Testament Prophecies for John the Baptizer". Klang Church of Christ. <http://klangchurchofchrist.org/three-old-testament-prophecies-of-john-the-baptizer>

Canfield, Jack. "How to discover your life purpose". <https://www.jackcanfield.com/blog/finding-life-purpose/>

Cranston, Robert E. "God uses flawed people." Christian Medical & Dental Associations. <https://cmda.org/god-uses-flawed-people/>

Cocherell, B.L. "Cyrus: God's anointed shepherd". <http://www.bible-prophecy.net/articles/a2pws.htm>

Department of Genetics and Genome Biology. "Genetic fingerprinting explained." University of Leicester. <https://www2.le.ac.uk/departments/genetics/jeffreys/explained>

Enlow, Johnny. "God told me "This is the end of the world as you know it"." 'It's Supernational' YouTube channel, hosted by Sid Roth. 17 August 2020. <https://www.youtube.com/watch?v=qkt5IP2mzuA>

Dale, Etta. "10 ways to stop negative self-talk." LiveLiving.org <https://www.liveliving.org/10-ways-to-stop-negative-self-talk/>

Explaining the Book (Bible Study Guide). "When did Jeremiah begin his ministry?" <https://www.explainingthebook.com/when-did-jeremiah-begin-his-ministry/>

Gause, Kara. "The Birth of John the Baptist Foretold". She Reads Truth. <https://shereadstruth.com/the-birth-of-john-the-baptist-foretold/>

Graves, Dan. "Who Was Timothy in the Bible? How Did He Help Paul?". Christianity.com <https://www.christianity.com/bible/people-of-the-bible/st-timothy-pauls-associate-11629587.html>

Houk, Sharon. "Why am I here on earth?" CBN.com. <https://www1.cbn.com/questions/why-am-i-here-on-earth>

Kahn, Ronnie. "Finding Purpose". AANA.com.au <https://aana.com.au/2019/12/02/finding-purpose/>

Kenneth Copeland Ministries. "3 ways to overcome unbelief." <https://blog.kcm.org/3-ways-overcome-unbelief/>

Kim, David. "Thy kingdom come – what it means and how to pray it." Pursuit Bible. <https://pursuitbible.com/thy-kingdom-come/>

Jackson, Wayne. "Cyrus the Great in Biblical Prophecy". Christian Courier. <https://www.christiancourier.com/articles/264-cyrus-the-great-in-biblical-prophecy>

Laws, Lori. "I don't want to create an Ishmael." LoriLaws.net <http://www.lorilaws.net/i-dont-want-to-create-an-ishmael/>

Lucey, Candice. "What 'let go and let God' does and does not mean for Christians. Crosswalk.com <https://www.crosswalk.com/faith/spiritual-life/what-let-go-and-let-god-does-and-does-not-mean-for-christians.html>

Mills, Michelle J. "Hammer-ing a new message". DaBelly.com. <http://www.dabelly.com/features/feature02.htm>

Olive Tree Blog. "What Does It Mean to Fear the Lord?" <https://www.olivetree.com/blog/what-does-it-mean-to-fear-the-lord/>

Simmons, William A. "John the Baptist". Bible Study Tools. <https://www.biblestudytools.com/dictionary/john-the-baptist/>

Stewart, Leigh. "5 scientific reasons why you are totally unique." Atlas. <https://atlasbiomed.com/blog/five-scientific-reasons-why-you-are-totally-unique/>

Swanson, Phillip J. "Occupations and Professions in the Bible". Studylight.org. <https://www.studylight.org/dictionaries/hbd/o/occupations-and-professions-in-the-bible.html>

Swindoll, Chuck. "Jeremiah". Insight for Living Ministries. <https://www.insight.org/resources/bible/the-major-prophets/jeremiah>

Thompson, Clive. "The myth of fingerprints." Smithsonian Magazine. <https://www.smithsonianmag.com/science-nature/myth-fingerprints-180971640/>

Towns, Dr Elmer. "What does the Bible say about personality?". Bible Sprout. <https://www.biblesprout.com/articles/bible/personality/>

Ward, Mike. "What is God's purpose for your life (and how to find it)?" Cornerstone University. 17 January 2017. <https://www.cornerstone.edu/blog-post/what-is-gods-purpose-for-your-life-and-how-to-find-it/>

Warren, Rick. "God doesn't force us; He gives us a choice." PastorRick.com. <https://pastorrick.com/god-doesnt-force-us-he-gives-us-a-choice/>

www.ingramcontent.com/pod-product-compliance
Lightning Source LLC
Chambersburg PA
CBHW051047050726
47592CB00002B/432